D0053389

THE LITERARY COMPANION

Emma Jones

A THINK BOOK FOR

ROBSON BOOKS

OTHER BOOKS IN THE COMPANION SERIES

The Cook's Companion
Edited by Jo Swinnerton
ISBN 1-86105-772-5

The Gardener's Companion
Edited by Vicky Bamforth
ISBN 1-86105-771-7

The London Companion
Edited by Jo Swinnerton
ISBN 1-86105-799-7

The Moviegoer's Companion
Edited by Rhiannon Guy
ISBN 1-86105-797-0

The Politics Companion
Edited by Matthew Stadlen and Harry Glass
ISBN 1-86105-796-2

The Traveller's Companion
Edited by Georgina Newbery and Rhiannon Guy
ISBN 1-86105-773-3

The Walker's Companion
Edited by Malcolm Tait
ISBN 1-86105-825-X

The Wildlife Companion
Edited by Malcolm Tait and Olive Tayler
ISBN 1-86105-770-9

SERIES EDITORS

Malcolm Tait, Emma Jones and Jo Swinnerton

Persons attempting to find a motive in this narrative will be prosecuted; persons attempting to find a moral in it will be banished; persons attempting to find a plot in it will be shot.

Mark Twain, Notice in *The Adventures of Huckleberry Finn*

THINK
A Think Book
for Robson Books

First published in Great Britain in 2004 by
Robson Books
The Chrysalis Building, Bramley Road, London W10 6SP

An imprint of **Chrysalis** Books Group plc

Text © Think Publishing 2004
Design and layout © Think Publishing 2004
The moral rights of the authors have been asserted

Edited by Emma Jones
The Companion team: Vicky Bamforth, James Collins, Charlie Furniss,
Harry Glass, Rhiannon Guy, Lou Millward, Matthew Stadlen,
Jo Swinnerton and Malcolm Tait

Think Publishing
The Pall Mall Deposit
124-128 Barlby Road, London W10 6BL
www.thinkpublishing.co.uk

All rights reserved. No part of this publication may be reproduced, stored
in a retrieval system, or transmitted in any form or by any means, electronic,
mechanical, photocopying, recording or otherwise, without the prior
permission of the copyright holder.
A CIP catalogue record for this book is available from the British Library.

ISBN 1-86105-798-9

Printed and bound in Italy by ▨ Grafica Veneta S.p.A.

The publishers and authors have made every effort to ensure the accuracy and
currency of the information in The Literary Companion. Similarly, every
effort has been made to contact copyright holders. We apologise for any
unintentional errors or omissions. The publisher and authors disclaim any
liability, loss, injury or damage incurred as a consequence, directly or
indirectly, of the use and application of the contents of this book.

The printing press is either the greatest blessing or the greatest curse of modern times, sometimes one forgets which it is.

JM Barrie

A WORD OF THANKS

This book would not have been possible without the
research, ideas, and dogged support of:

Dominic Bates, Paul Bates, Adam Biles, Sarah Bove,
Suzanne Carmichael, Haf Cennydd, Suzanne Cullen,
Stuart Fance, Kim Gifford, Lucy Grewcock, Ivo Grigorov,
Lisa Holm, Nikki Illes, Larry Langford, Delphine Lecourtois,
Dominic, Katie, Rachel, Tony and Diane Jones,
Charli Morgan, Julie Riches, Jennifer Styles and
Nathalie Stahelin.

There were only, it has been said, three stories ever written. Boy meets girl. Boy loses girl. Man hunts whale. Everything you ever read or write is no more than a derivation or combination of these.

Well, at last comes the book to give the lie to that theory. Liberally scattered throughout this volume of literary luminaries, novelistic niceties and poetic polemics are more, many more than just three tales. For *The Literary Companion* tells the stories behind the stories.

And what stories they are. You'll find out more about Dickens and Chaucer, Keats and Amis than their books could ever tell you. It works the other way round, too. You'll also find out more about *Oliver Twist* and *The Canterbury Tales*, 'Ode to a Nightingale' and *Lucky Jim* than their authors could ever tell you.

For *The Literary Companion* is far more than just a trivia guide (although if you do tuck it down your sock at the next pub quiz, then that tenner is yours). It opens the portals of the wide world of literature, from the pens that scribble it to the libraries that house it, and every painstakingly crafted phrase in between. It will make you laugh, it will raise your eyebrows, and it will draw you even further into the literary minds that have enriched our ages.

Your bookshelf will never be the same.

Emma Jones, Editor

READING BY NUMBERS

Ten Little Indians, Agatha Christie (1939)
The Nine Tailors, Dorothy Leigh Sayers (1966)
Eight Cousins, Louisa May Alcott (1874)
The Seven Sisters, Margaret Drabble (2002)
Six Characters in Search of an Author, Luigi Pirandello (1921)
Slaughterhouse-Five, Kurt Vonnegut (1969)
The Sign of Four, Arthur Conan Doyle (1890)
Three Men in a Boat, Jerome K Jerome (1889)
A Tale of Two Cities, Charles Dickens (1859)
One Flew Over the Cuckoo's Nest, Ken Kesey (1962)
And Then There Were None, Agatha Christie (1939)

QUOTE UNQUOTE

A man's got to take a lot of punishment to write a really funny book.
Ernest Hemingway, US novelist

TALES OF THE UNEXPECTED

In *Gulliver's Travels* (1726) Jonathan Swift wrote of 'two lesser stars, or satellites, which revolve about Mars; whereof the innermost is distant from the centre of the primary planet exactly three of his diameters, and the outermost, five; the former revolves in the space of ten hours, and the latter in twenty-one and a half; so that the squares of their periodical times are very near in the same proportion with the cubes of their distance from the centre of Mars; which evidently shows them to be governed by the same law of gravitation that influences the other heavenly bodies'.

He had described almost exactly the two moons of Mars more than 150 years before they were discovered.

ANAGRAM ANARCHY

Richard Wallace, author of *Jack the Ripper, Light Hearted Friend* (1996), spent years examining what he perceived to be hidden anagrams in Lewis Carroll's poetry in an effort to prove that the author was the killer. He 'translated' such lines as 'Twas brillig, and the slithy toves/ Did gyre and gimble in the wabe/ All mimsy were the borogoves/ And the mome raths outgrabe' from *Jabberwocky* into such gibberish as 'Bet I beat my glands til/ With hand-sword I slay the evil gender/ A slimey theme; borrow gloves/ and masturbate the hog more!' For Ripperologists, it's the literary equivalent of playing Ozzy Osbourne LPs backwards and hearing: 'Hi, I'm Satan, how are you?'

LITERARY FESTIVITIES

When Hay-on-Wye's first secondhand bookshop opened in 1961, it started something of a trend. In this tiny town there are now 39 bookshops for 1,300 residents (that's one shop for every 34 people) and a contagious literary hay fever that culminates in late May with the 10-day programme of talks, interviews, lectures, concerts and workshops that is **The Guardian Hay Festival** (www.hayfestival.com).

The Hay has fans in high places: politician and diarist Tony Benn enjoys it so much he once said, 'For me, it has replaced Christmas.' Bill Clinton famously named it the 'Woodstock of the mind' when he was controversially paid to appear in 2001. But no one is completely certain whether he was talking about the meet or the weather – downpours of near Biblical proportions hit the festival every year.

CHEMICAL FICTION

Rudyard Kipling may have claimed that words are the greatest drug known to man, but legions of other writers have selflessly dedicated themselves to proving him wrong. Here are a few titles to expand your mind as well as your bookshelf...

Alice's Adventures in Wonderland (1865, debated), Lewis Carroll
Cocaine Nights (1996, cocaine), JG Ballard
The Confessions of an English Opium Eater (1821, opium),
Thomas de Quincy
The Doors of Perception (1954, mescaline), Aldous Huxley
The Electric Kool-Aid Acid Test (1968, LSD), Tom Wolfe
Fear and Loathing in Las Vegas (1971, anything imaginable),
Hunter S Thompson
Glamorama (1998, cocaine), Bret Easton Ellis
Junky (1953, heroin), William Burroughs (under
the pen name William Lee)
Kubla Khan (1797, opium), Samuel Taylor Coleridge
Powder (1999, cocaine), Kevin Sampson
The Teachings of Don Juan (1969, mescaline), Carlos Casteneda
Trainspotting (1993, heroin), Irvine Welsh
Under the Volcano (1947, mescaline), Malcolm Lowry

TAKE A BREAK

Victor Hugo's *Les Misérables* (1862) contains one of the longest sentences in the French language. The author crafted a barely readable 823 words before finally hitting the breathless reader with a full stop.

Age, in his life, at which Jean Paul Sartre's autobiography, 11
the Nobel Prize-winning Les Mots *(1964), ends*

AMAZONIAN BOOKSTORES

The world's largest bookshop is the Barnes & Noble Bookstore, New York City, USA. It has over 12 miles of shelving and covers an area of around 14,500 square metres. Waterstones in Piccadilly, London is the largest in Europe, while Amazon.com, with its catalogue of 4.7 million books, is the largest online bookshop in the world.

QUOTE UNQUOTE

Outside of a dog, a book is man's best friend.
Inside of a dog it's too dark to read.
Groucho Marx, US humorist

DIGITAL LITERATURE

Just as it is impossible to determine when the wheel was invented or who had the inspiration to suggest that flesh might taste better were it warmed up a little, the exact moment of the ebook's conception is already hotly contested. Some credit Jim Sachs (the inventor of the computer mouse) with this honour, citing the Softbook he developed in his garage in 1995 – from acrylic sheeting and sprinkler tubes – as the giant leap for readers everywhere.

At the same time, however, in the skies above Detroit, Daniel Munyan was furiously making notes. Seeing the discomfort of a fellow passenger who was struggling to angle his reading light, Munyan had a moment of inspiration and dreamt up the Everybook in all its digital literary glory. Both were unaware of the Sony Bookman, a digital reading device launched to little fanfare in the USA in 1992.

Referring both to the digital viewing device itself and the text file, the ebook follows in a long tradition of attempts to condense as much text as possible into the smallest physical space. Whether ebooks succeed where miniature manuscripts and microfiches have failed, however, will depend on their acceptance by the public at large. The co-operation of several high-profile authors, including Dean Koontz and Stephen King, can only help in this respect, as will the proliferation of 'pirated' novel transcripts that can be located easily online and the increasing versatility of mobile telephones and PDAs.

Yet perhaps the biggest challenge for those who wish to replace the print and paper in our lives with microchips and LCD (liquid crystal display) is to develop an ebook viewer that can not only hold 25 novels in its databanks, but which is equally effective at stopping doors and squashing flies.

12 *Number of draft pages Beryl Bainbridge estimates she writes for every page that gets into print*

Wannabe authors take note! If repeated rejection by publishing houses becomes too much for you to take, you might want to consider self-publishing. You'll have to have a fair amount put aside. A print run that includes project management, critical appraisal, type setting, ISBN registration, cover design, barcode origination, printing, warehousing and even an optional rewrite service could cost anywhere between £3,000 and £8,000.

A quick search online yields plenty of companies willing to assist in your literary quest. But, self-publication is only the beginning and without a distribution deal, getting those 1,000 newly printed copies of experimental literature onto high-street shelves requires a sharp business sense and an even sharper tongue. Sadly, more often than not, such attempts will end in disappointment.

However, it's not all doom and gloom. Take Reverend Graham Taylor of Cloughton, North Yorkshire. Frustrated by successive rejection of *Shadowmancer* – a tale of black magic and Christianity in the seventeenth century – he sold the motorbike he used to visit parishioners and funded its publication at a cost of £3,500. After persuading a major high-street chain to stock copies, his book was spotted and published by Faber UK. A few months later, the book had become a children's bestseller, at which point an American publisher bought the rights for $500,000. There is still no word on whether Reverend Taylor has since replaced his motorcycle.

COMEDIANS ON READING

I was in Nashville, Tennesee, last year. After the show I went to a Waffle House. I'm not proud of it, I was hungry. And I'm alone, I'm eating and I'm reading a book, right? Waitress walks over to me, 'Tch tch tch tch. Hey, what you readin' for?' Is that like the weirdest fucking question you've ever heard? Not what am I reading, but what am I reading for. Well, godammit, you stumped me. Why do I read? Well... hmmm... I guess I read for a lot of reasons, and the main one is so I don't end up being a fucking waffle waitress.

Bill Hicks, *Revelations*

POETIC PUZZLERS

Unscramble these well-known writers

DO HASTY HARM • MY NOBLE RITE
TOILETS • NO LEGAL PARADE

Answer on page 153.

Lord of the Jives
A group of shipwrecked Scots decide who will be ruler of the island in a Gaelic dance-off. Ralph wins and is crowned Lord of the Jives; Piggy loses and is killed in a group riverdance.

HUMP-BACK RIDER

Humping books around can be a tiring business so spare a thought for the 400 camels of Abdul Kassem Ismael of Persia. This tenth-century scholarly grand vizier never left home without his personal library of 117,000 volumes, and to ensure his librarians could locate any book almost immediately, the animals were trained to walk in alphabetical order. It all sheds new light on Rudyard Kipling's description in the *Just So Stories* of how the camel got his hump because he spent his days saying 'humph'.

14 *Area, in thousands of square feet, of the oldest bookshop in America – the Moravian Book Shop in Pennsylvania*

Emma has been meaning to read more ever since she was twelve years old. I have seen a great many lists of her drawing-up at various times of books that she meant to read regularly through – and very good lists they were – very well chosen, and very neatly arranged – sometimes alphabetically, and sometimes by some other rule. The list she drew up when only fourteen – I remember thinking it did her judgment so much credit, that I preserved it some time; and I dare say she may have made out a very good list now. But I have done with expecting any course of steady reading from Emma. She will never submit to any thing requiring industry and patience, and a subjection of the fancy to the understanding. Where Miss Taylor failed to stimulate, I may safely affirm that Harriet Smith will do nothing – you never could persuade her to read half so much as you wished – you know you could not.

Jane Austen, Emma

BOOKS BEFORE THE BIG TIME

It's a rare writer who makes it big on their first book. Here are some of the first offerings of some of our favourite authors...

John Berger, *A Painter of Our Time* (1958)

Angela Carter, *Shadow Dance* (1966)

Wilkie Collins, *Antonina* (1850)

Joseph Conrad, *Almayer's Folly* (1895)

Charles Dickens, *Sketches by Boz* (1836)

George Eliot, *Scenes of Clerical Life* (1858)

F Scott Fitzgerald, *This Side of Paradise* (1920)

EM Forster, *Where Angels Fear to Tread* (1905)

George Gissing, *Workers in the Dawn* (1880)

Thomas Hardy, *Desperate Remedies* (1871)

Jerome K Jerome, *On the Stage – and Off* (1885)

James Joyce, *Chamber Music* (1907)

DH Lawrence, *The White Peacock* (1911)

Iris Murdoch, *Sartre: Romantic Rationalist* (1953)

Sir Walter Scott, *The Lay of the Last Minstrel* (1805)

Robert Louis Stevenson, *An Inland Voyage* (1878)

Bram Stoker, *The Primrose Path* (1875)

Anthony Trollope, *The Macdermots of Ballycloran* (1847)

Herman Melville, *Typee, a Peep at Polynesian Life* (1846)

The Chinese discovered how to make paper in the first century AD. But while they were happy to distribute paper throughout the Asian and Arab worlds, they kept knowledge of its manufacture a closely guarded secret. The news finally got out when an Arab army captured an entire town full of paper makers at the Battle of Talas in 751.

The first words were printed in Chinese temples in the second century AD using engraved marble columns. Pilgrims visiting the temple could print their own Sutras off the columns onto damp pieces of paper.

By the sixth century, Chinese printers had developed engraved wood blocks to print manuscripts. Surviving fragments of Buddhist incantations show this technology had reached Japan in the eighth century, and the world's oldest surviving book, *Jin gang ban ruo bo luo mi jing*, or *The Diamond Sutra*, was printed in 868.

In the eleventh century, a Chinese alchemist called Pi Sheng invented movable, reusable type. Pi Sheng's invention was not popular in China and moveable type didn't really take off until Korean King Htai Tjong ordered the first set of 100,000 pieces of type to be cast in bronze in 1403. Nine further fonts were to be developed before Europe discovered typography.

German goldsmith Johannes Gensfleisch zur Laden zum Gutenberg is the father of European printing. He modelled his printing press on wine-pressing techniques and his inks were made from a combination of boiled linseed oil and soot. *The Gutenberg Bibles*, the first mass-produced books and the oldest surviving example of printing with movable metal type, were published on 23 February 1455.

It was only after William Caxton learnt the trade while in Flanders that printing began in England. He established the first English press in Westminster in 1476, and printed *Dictes or Sayengis of the Philosophres*, the first book ever printed in English, in 1477.

In 1534, Henry VIII granted Cambridge University the rights to establish its own press, making it the first printing and publishing house in the world. Its rival, Oxford University Press, is the world's largest university press. Its first book was printed in 1478, only two years after Caxton established his press in Westminster. However, its right to print books wasn't set in stone until 1586.

In 1876, Mark Twain made publishing history when *The Adventures of Tom Sawyer* became the first typewritten manuscript ever to be delivered to a publisher. The typewriter? An 1874 Remington, perfected from Christopher Sholes's 1819 invention.

The date, in June 1904, on which Stephen Dedalus and Leopold Bloom make their epic journeys through Dublin in James Joyce's Ulysses *(1922)*

PULPED FICTION

When engineers started searching for a suitably absorbent pulp to lay on the M6 toll motorway in 2003, they found it at an unexpectedly slushy publishing company. The pulp was needed to strengthen the tarmac and create a long-lasting soundproof layer, and the books they found most suitable were Mills and Boon romantic novels.

About 2,500,000 old copies were pulped and mixed into the road's top layer – that's about 45,000 books for every mile of Britain's first pay-as-you-go motorway. Mills and Boon were chosen because of the books' super-absorbent qualities. 'They may be slushy to many people, but it's their 'no-slushiness' that is their attraction as far as we are concerned,' Brian Kent from Tarmac told the BBC.

HOW TO READ

*'Begin at the beginning, and go on till you
come to the end; then stop.'*

These simple instructions are given by the King of Hearts to the White Rabbit in Lewis Carroll's *Alice's Adventures in Wonderland* (1865) when the rabbit is called up to testify against the Knave of Hearts (who has been accused of stealing tarts). The King's advice is less nonsensical than it first seems; the rabbit is reading from a piece of paper containing verses with no beginning, no end – and no meaning.

ON THE ROAD

Books shouldn't be trapped on overcrowded and dusty bookshelves nor reserved for just one reader, not according to www.bookcrossing.com at any rate. They believe our books should be set free 'into the wild' so they can spread their joy to all those who weren't prepared enough to pack their own books for the train ride to work.

US software and internet guru, Ron Hornbaker founded the organisation in 2001. It already has more than 250,000 members 'releasing' and 'capturing' registered books at assorted locations worldwide. It works something like this: you register online (free) and pick up a code (free), after you've finished your latest catch, you jot down the code and set it free (free). The person who picks it up (free), logs onto the website (free) and posts you a lovely message about how nice it was of you to leave the book and where they had last left it (for free). Bargain.

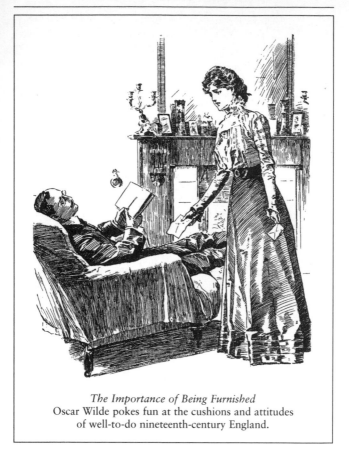

The Importance of Being Furnished
Oscar Wilde pokes fun at the cushions and attitudes
of well-to-do nineteenth-century England.

HOLY COW

You might think that an author tends to write about subjects he knows well. Not so with Oliver Goldsmith who remarkably chose to write books on subjects of which he happily admitted to knowing nothing. One of these was *The History of the Earth and Animated Nature* (1774), about which Samuel Johnson wrote: 'If he could tell a horse from a cow that was the extent of his knowledge of zoology; and yet [it] can still be read with pleasure from the charm of the author's style'.

If you were asked where John Steinbeck took his inspiration for *The Winter of Our Discontent*, you'd probably know the answer (Shakespeare, *Richard III*), but what about the following 'adopted' titles:

Far from the Madding Crowd, Thomas Hardy
From *Elegy Written in a Country Churchyard* by Thomas Gray
'Far from the madding crowd's ignoble strife
Their sober wishes never learned to stray.'

Cakes and Ale, W Somerset Maugham
From Shakespeare's *Twelfth Night*, Act II, scene iii
'Sir Toby Belch: Dost thou think, because thou art virtuous, there
shall be no more cakes and ale?'

For Whom the Bell Tolls, Ernest Hemingway
From 'Meditation XVII – No Man is an Island' by John Donne
'...any man's death diminishes me, because I am involved in
mankind; and therefore never send to know for whom the bell tolls;
it tolls for thee.'

The Darling Buds of May, HE Bates
From the Shakespeare sonnet
'Shall I compare thee to a summer's day?
Thou art more lovely and more temperate.
Rough winds do shake the darling buds of May
And summer's lease hath all too short a date.'

Of Mice and Men, John Steinbeck
From *To a Mouse* by Robert Burns
'The best laid schemes o'mice an' men, Gang aft a-gley'

Brave New World, Aldous Huxley
From Shakespeare's *The Tempest*, Act V, scene i
'Miranda: How beauteous mankind is! O brave new world
That has such people in't!'

The Power and the Glory, Graham Greene
From the Bible, Matthew 6:9
'For thine is the kingdom, and the power,
and the glory, for ever, amen.'

The Sound and the Fury, William Faulkner
From Shakespeare's *Macbeth*, Act V, scene v
'Macbeth: It is a tale
Told by an idiot, full of sound and fury,
Signifying nothing.'

A Handful of Dust, Evelyn Waugh
From TS Eliot's *The Wasteland*
'I will show you fear in a handful of dust.'

CEASE THIS DETESTABLE
BOO-HOOING INSTANTLY!

As befitting an author who penned an entire play on the pleasures of bringing correct English phonetics to the masses, George Bernard Shaw left a bizarre will bequeathing his worldly goods to the development of a rational spelling system, which wasn't resolved until 1999, almost half a century after his death. The will, which named the National Gallery in Dublin, the Royal Academy of Dramatic Art, and the British Museum as beneficiaries of the remaining fortune, prompted decades of parliamentary debates, threats of legal action, and discord between the organisations which weren't to receive a penny until the English language was reformed.

When an out-of-court settlement awarded a one-off payment towards a book on phonetic spelling, the dispute appeared settled until the British Library got in on the act. They argued that it was the library (which had split from the museum in 1972) that was Shaw's intended beneficiary, since he had acknowledged in his will 'the incalculable value to me of my daily resort to the reading room of the institution at the beginning of my career'. The quarrel was finally resolved in 1999 when the two agreed to share the £7 million inheritance.

POETIC PUZZLERS

**Four writers joined by one furtive theme.
Name the link...**

Ian Fleming • Grahame Greene
Christopher Marlowe • W Somerset Maugham

Answer on page 153.

BOOKSHOP STORIES

Established in 1953 by poet Lawrence Ferlinghetti and Peter D Martin, City Lights was America's first all-paperback bookstore. Based at 261 Columbus Avenue, San Francisco, the store began its long association with the writers of the Beat Generation when, in 1955, Ferlinghetti launched his *Pocket Poets* Series.

In 1956, City Lights fought an obscenity lawsuit for publishing Allen Ginsberg's *Howl and Other Poems*. Ferlinghetti staked everything on the outcome of the trial, and to lose could have meant bankruptcy. However, the judge concluded that if a work of art had social worth (and *Howl*, he argued, did) then it couldn't be classed as obscene. Ferlinghetti left court both victorious and notorious, the future of City Lights secured.

BRINGING OUT THE BIG BUCKS

Mary Higgens Clark, 'America's Queen of Suspense' was paid £45 million for a five-book deal with Simon & Schuster.

A two-book deal with Penguin Puttnam earned **Tom Clancy**, author of *The Hunt for Red October*, £32 million.

HarperCollins paid **Michael Crichton**, creator of *Jurassic Park* and *ER*, £27 million for a two-book deal.

Stephen King received £23 million for his final four-book deal before he announced he was giving up writing.

Barbara Taylor Bradford, author of *A Woman of Substance*, was given £20 million for a three-book deal in 1994.

After the huge success of his American Civil War novel *Cold Mountain,* **Charles Frazier** was paid $8 million for his second book on the basis of a one-page outline. That's a large leap from the $100,000 he was offered for *Cold Mountain* in the mid-1990s.

JK Rowling earned herself an advance of £2 million for the *Harry Potter* series. She was paid just £2,500 for the first Harry Potter book.

Another £2 million went to **Nicholas Evans** for his first novel, *The Horse Whisperer*, after furious bidding on the manuscript at the Frankfurt Book Fair.

After the success of his best-selling novels *High Fidelity* and *Fever Pitch,* **Nick Hornby** received £2 million for two books on moving to Penguin.

Hari Kunzru received £1.25 million for UK, American and European rights on publication of his debut novel *The Impressionist* in 2002.

The largest amount ever to be given to an unknown author (£700,000) went to **Eoin Colfer** for *Artemis Fowl*, 'the new Harry Potter'.

Joan Collins holds the record for the largest unreturned advance. The actress retained the $1.2 million advance for *A Ruling Passion* after Random House refused the draft as 'dull', 'cliched' and 'unsatisfactory'. The publisher sued for the return of the money, but in 1996, the New York State Supreme Court ruled that Collins had fulfilled her contract and could keep the cash. The novel remains unpublished.

YOUNG BLOOD

'J' is the youngest letter in the English alphabet, it wasn't added until the 1600s when it grew out of the letter 'i' as its capital form.

WRITERS ON READING

As a nation grows and changes, its literature grows and changes with it. At first it asks only for stories, then it asks for history for its own sake, and for poetry for its own sake; history, I mean, for the knowledge it gives us of the past; poetry for joy in the beautiful words, and not merely for the stories they tell. Then, as a nation's needs and knowledge grow, it demands ever more and more books on all kinds of subjects.

And we ourselves grow and change just as a nation does. When we are very young, there are many books which seem to us dull and stupid. But as we grow older and learn more, we begin to like more and more kinds of books. We may still love the stories that we loved as children, but we love others too. And at last, perhaps, there comes a time when those books which seemed to us most dull and stupid delight us the most.

HE Marshall, *English Literature for Boys and Girls*

QUOTE UNQUOTE

Reading is not a duty, and has consequently no business to be made disagreeable.
Augustine Birrell, British literary wit and politician

LITERARY PRIZES

Hungarian-born American journalist Joseph Pulitzer established the Pulitzer Prize as an incentive to excellence in his 1904 will. Prizes in literature were to go to an American novel, an original American play performed in New York, a book on the history of the United States, an American biography, and a history of public service by the press. Since the prizes were launched in 1917, the judging panel has increased the number of awards to 21 and introduced poetry as a subject in the literature category. The prizes are awarded each April by the President of Columbia University.

Only two winners have turned down the prize: Sinclair Lewis for *Arrowsmith* in 1926 (novel) and William Saroyan for *The Time of Your Life* in 1940 (drama). Lewis refused the prize saying he believed that the Pulitzer was meant for books that celebrated American wholesomeness and his novels, which were critical, should not be considered; Saroyan turned his down saying that art could not be patronised by wealth. At $7,500 a pop, he was making a pretty big point.

John F Kennedy is the only US President to be awarded a Pulitzer Prize. He was presented with the 1957 Pulitzer Prize in Biography for *Profiles in Courage*.

22 *Number of days Jeffrey Archer spent in HMP Belmarsh, a high-security prison that houses some of Britain's most violent criminals*

BOOKS TO BAWL TO

Read'em and weep...

After You'd Gone, Maggie O'Farrell (2000)
The Amber Spyglass, Philip Pullman (2000)
A River Runs through It, Norman MacLean (1976)
Doctor Zhivago, Boris Pasternak (1957)
Flowers for Algernon, Daniel Keyes (1966)
Gone with the Wind, Margaret Mitchell (1936)
Jane Eyre, Charlotte Brontë (1847)
Little Women, Louisa May Alcott (1868)
The Lovely Bones, Alice Sebold (2002)
Rebecca, Daphne du Maurier (1938)
Sophie's Choice, William Styron (1979)
The Tin Drum, Günter Grass (1959)
Watership Down, Richard Adams (1972)
The World According to Garp, John Irving (1978)

QUOTE UNQUOTE

I would sooner read a timetable or a catalog than nothing at all.
W Somerset Maugham, novelist

LOST IN TRANSLATION

Book titles that don't work quite so well in the 21st century...

American Bottom Archaeology (Anon, 1983)
The Big Book of Busts (John Watson and Eric Schiller, 1994)
British Tits (Christopher M Perrins, 1979)
Enid Blyton's Gay Story Book (Enid Blyton, 1957)
Flashes from the Welsh Pulpit (J Gwnoro Davies, 1889)
Games You Can Play With Your Pussy (Ira Alterman, 1885)
Alterman can also be thanked for: *Sex Manual For People Over 30,
Do Diapers Give You Leprosy?*, *Games for the John* and *A Man in
the Hand is Worth Two in the Bush*.
The Hookers' Art (Jesse A Turbayne, 1993)
How to Mount Deer for Profit or Fun (Archie Phillips, 1980)
'Invisible Dick' the boy superhero in *Sparky* (1960)
The Romance of the Beaver (A Radclyffe Dugmore, 1914)
Scouts in Bondage (Boy Scouts Association, 1930)
The Scrubber Strategy (Baviello, Bowie and Beerman, 1982)
Shag the Caribou (C Bernard Rutley, 1943)
Whippings and Lashings (Girl Guide Association, 1970)

Number of prisoners guillotined in Charles Dickens' A Tale of Two Cities. 23
Sydney Carton (standing in for protagonist Charles Darney) is the 23rd man

BRIGHT YOUNG THINGS

In 1979, *The Observer* published a list of 80 young people they predicted would define the country's culture, politics and economics for a generation. They repeated the exercise in 2004, these are the few writers who made the final cut:

Hari Kunzru (novelist)
Martin McDonagh (playwright)
Alice Oswald (poet)
Helen Walsh (author)
Sarah Waters (novelist)
Louise Welsh (author)

UNGODLY ERRORS

The 'Wicked Bible'
In a fifteenth-century edition of the King James Bible, the word 'not' was accidentally omitted from the seventh commandment, so that it actually encouraged readers to commit adultery. The copies were recalled immediately (dashing the hopes of many).

The 'Fool's Bible'
A 1632 print-run made a similar boob. They replaced 'no' with 'a' in Psalm 14 to read: 'The Fool hath said in his heart there is a God.' The resulting fine put the printing house out of business.

The 'Unrighteous Bible'
The word 'not' was also omitted in a later 1653 edition, but this time in Corinthians VI to read: 'Know ye not that the unrighteous shall inherit the Kingdom of God', much to the consternation of all do-gooders.

The 'Printer's Bible'
In a 1702 version, the printing house must have been subconsciously aware of the ramifications of error. They substituted the word 'printers' for 'princes' in Psalm 119 to read: 'printers have persecuted me'.

The 'Sinner's Bible'
Ten years later and an Irish edition was commanding the faithful to 'sin on more', replacing the 'sin no more' that is generally preferred by practising Christians.

The 'Murderer's Bible'
The word 'murmurers' was replaced with 'murderers' in an 1801 print-run. 'Let the children first be killed' (for 'filled'), it bloodthirstily continued.

The 'Lion's Bible'
'Loins' became 'lions' in an 1804 edition to read rather confusingly: 'thy son that shall come forth out of thy lions'.

The 'He Bible'
A 1923 edition more than stated the obvious when it got the sexes mixed up: 'A man may not marry his grandmother's wife', it sternly advised.

CREATIVE COCK-UPS

If Herman Melville ever wondered why the first edition of his novel *Moby-Dick* (1851) failed to sell well in Britain, he needed look no further than the last page. His all-important conclusion – you know, that little bit about Ishmael surviving the attack of the white whale – had been mislaid in transit, leading reviewers to slam the book for its hasty and unsatisfactory conclusion, and readers to throw their books down in despair at the unhappy tale.

THE NATION'S FAVOURITE POEMS

As voted by the British public for National Poetry Day in 1995

1. *If*, Rudyard Kipling
2. *The Lady of Shalott,* Alfred Lord Tennyson
3. *The Listeners*, Walter de la Mare
4. *Not Waving But Drowning,* Stevie Smith
5. *The Daffodils*, William Wordsworth
6. *To Autumn*, John Keats
7. *The Lake Isle of Innisfree,* WB Yeats
8. *Dulce et decorum est*, Wilfred Owen
9. *Ode to a Nightingale*, John Keats
10. *He Wishes for the Cloths of Heaven,* WB Yeats

HOW TO READ

Every extreme has its opposite, and speed-reading is no exception. The 'Slow Reading Movement' (much like the 'Slow Food Movement' except that it aims to decrease the speed of your eyes rather than that of your mouth) is the advocate of savouring the written word at a more leisurely pace.

The currently underground movement (it presumably takes a bit of time to read the manifesto) traces the idea back to the words of Nietzche who wrote of the idea of 'teaching slow reading' in the preface to *Daybreak* (1881): 'In the midst of an age of "work", that is to say, of hurry, of indecent and perspiring haste, which wants to "get everything done" at once, including every old or new book: this art does not so easily get anything done, it teaches to read WELL, that is to say, to read slowly, deeply, looking cautiously before and aft, with reservations, with doors left open, with delicate eyes and fingers.'

The cause offers a great excuse for not finishing the novel that's been sat on your bedside table since last Christmas, but you might look pretty simple staring at the same page for half an hour on the train to work.

THE REWRITE WAS BETTER

It is a truth universally acknowledged, that a single man in possession of a good fortune must be in want of a knife.

A 30-YEAR RIDDLE

'Why is a raven like a writing desk?'
'I haven't the slightest idea'

The Mad Hatter puts forward both this riddle and its lack of an answer at his tea party in Lewis Carroll's *Alice's Adventures in Wonderland* (1865). It caused so much frustrated conjecture that 30 years later, Carroll published the following solution in the preface to the 1896 edition: 'Because it can produce a few notes, tho they are very flat, and it is never put with the wrong end in front!' However, in 1976, Carroll-admirer Denis Crutch pointed out that in the original preface, Carroll had actually written: 'It is *nevar* put with the wrong end in front' (raven spelt backwards), which had been mistakenly corrected by proofreaders.

A READING RAINBOW

Red Badge of Courage – Stephen Crane (1895)
A Clockwork Orange – Anthony Burgess (1962)
Chrome Yellow – Aldous Huxley (1921)
How Green was my Valley – Richard Llewellyn (1939)
The Blue Bird – Maeterlinck (1909)
The Indigo Children – Lee Carroll and Jan Tober (1999)
Prater Violet – Christopher Isherwood (1945)
The Rainbow – DH Lawrence (1915)

TAKE ME TO YOUR LEADER

No suspension of disbelief was required on Halloween, 30 October 1938. The US radio-listening public fell for it hook, line and sinker when the cool, calm voice of Orson Welles boomed out through the speakers to tell an alarmed nation that the aliens had landed and that they hadn't come in peace. It may seem hard to believe today, but the first airing of the radio version of HG Wells' *The War of the Worlds*, caused such widespread panic that the police headquarters in Trenton, close to the fictional scene, recorded an onslaught of calls: 'Between 8:30pm and 10pm received numerous phone calls as result of WABC broadcast this evening re: Mars attacking this country. Calls included papers, police depts including NYC and private persons... At least 50 calls were answered. Persons calling inquiring as to meteors, number of persons killed, gas attack, military being called out and fires. All were advised nothing unusual had occurred and that rumors were due to a radio dramatization of a play.'

Welles appeared apologetic before the assembled press the next morning (although he later took full credit for the play's effect in a BBC interview in 1955), but writer HG Wells was seething. The script was such a loose adaptation of the original that Wells demanded a retraction ('Or I will blast you with my deadly heat-ray gun,' were apparently not his words).

QUOTE UNQUOTE

Writing today is like standing stark naked in Trafalgar Square and being told to get an erection.
Louis de Bernières, novelist, on the pressures of writing a follow up to a bestselling novel

GONE WITH THE WIND

After 50 years of speculation, the mysterious death of children's author and aristocratic adventurer Antoine de Saint-Exupéry finally came a step closer to being resolved when traces of his Lockheed Lightning P-38 turned up in the Mediterranean near Marseilles in 2004. The writer of dreamy classic *The Little Prince* (*Le Petit Prince*) had vanished without a trace on 31 July 1944, during an Allied reconnaissance mission, with some even claiming that he'd headed back to the Sahara to hook up with the book's time-travelling hero. As the evidence seems to suggest the crash was an accident, the news might well prompt a name change for the Aéroport Antoine de Saint-Exupéry in his home town of Lyon.

The fact of the matter is that the passage of time has driven a nail into the coffin of the carefully-crafted words of a select few. In a nutshell, and not to mince words, the following have taken the bull by its horns to stand head and shoulders above the rest...

Cloudcuckooland
Aristophanes (c.444 BC–380 BC), *Birds*. The word (in its closest rendition from Greek to English) comes up as a suggestion for the name of the capital city of birds.

All hell broke loose
John Milton, *Paradise Lost* (1667)

The law is an ass
Charles Dickens, *Oliver Twist* (1837–1838)

Boys will be boys
Anthony Hope, *The Dolly Dialogues* (1894)

The female of the species is more deadly than the male
Rudyard Kipling, 'The Female of the Species' (1911)

'Tis better to have loved and lost than never to have loved at all
Tennyson, *In Memoriam* (1850)

Funny peculiar or funny-ha-ha?
Ian Hay, *The Housemaster* (1936)

A dark horse
Benjamin Disraeli, *The Young Duke* (1831)
When originally used, it applied literally to a dark horse which had unexpectedly won a race: 'A dark horse which had never been thought of... rushed past the grandstand in sweeping triumph.'

That's the long and short of it
WS Gilbert, *Princess Ida* (1884)
Most probably influenced by Shakespeare's 'the short and the long of it', spoken by Mistress Quickly in *The Merry Wives of Windsor*.

Every dog has his day
George Borrow, *Lavengro* (1851)

As fresh as [is] the month of May
Geoffrey Chaucer, *The Canterbury Tales, Prologue* (c.1387)

I'm no angel
Although some consider it to have originated with Mae West, it was actually first used by Becky Sharp in William M Thackeray's *Vanity Fair* (1848)

No time like the present
Mrs Manley, *The Lost Lover* (1696)

So near and yet so far
Tennyson, *In Memoriam* (1850)

Variety is the spice of life
William Cowper, *The Task* (1785)

Ignorance is bliss
Thomas Gray, *Ode on a Distant Prospect of Eton College* (1742)

Thanks for nothing
From 'Thank you for nothing', Cervantes, *Don Quixote* (1605)

LITERARY PHOBIAS

Scared of reading or saying long words? Then you possibly suffer from (but will probably never be able to read or say) 'hipomonsteresquipedalophobia', the phobia of long words. Other linguistic phobias include 'graphophobia', the fear of looking at writing, 'sophophobia', the fear of learning (a likely story) and 'verbophobia', the fear of words.

POETIC PUZZLERS

**Four writers joined by one chugging theme.
Name the link and the titles...**

Agatha Christie • Michael Crichton
Graham Greene • E Nesbit
Answer on page 153.

WRITERS ON READING

I am so great a lover of and believer in fairy tales that I once organized a society for the dissemination of fairy literature, and at the first meeting of this society we resolved to demand of the board of education to drop mathematics from the curriculum in the public schools and to substitute therefor a four years' course in fairy literature, to be followed, if the pupil desired, by a post-graduate course in demon ology and folk-lore. We hired and fitted up large rooms, and the cause seemed to be flourishing until the second month's rent fell due. It was then discovered that the treasury was empty; and with this discovery the society ended its existence, without having accomplished any tangible result other than the purchase of a number of sofas and chairs, for which Judge Methuen and I had to pay.

Still, I am of the opinion (and Judge Methuen indorses it) that we need in this country of ours just that influence which the fairy tale exerts. We are becoming too practical; the lust for material gain is throttling every other consideration. Our babes and sucklings are no longer regaled with the soothing tales of giants, ogres, witches, and fairies; their hungry, receptive minds are filled with stories about the pursuit and slaughter of unoffending animals, of war and of murder, and of those questionable practices whereby a hero is enriched and others are impoverished. Before he is out of his swaddling-cloth the modern youngster is convinced that the one noble purpose in life is to get, get, get, and keep on getting of worldly material.

The fairy tale is tabooed because, as the sordid parent alleges, it makes youth unpractical.

Eugene Field, *The Love Affairs Of A Bibliomaniac*

Africa
A Good Man in Africa,
William Boyd
The Famished Road, Ben Okri
A Year in Marrakesh,
Peter Mayne
Out of Africa, Karen Blixen
Heart of Darkness,
Joseph Conrad

Australia
The Songlines, Bruce Chatwin
Oscar and Lucinda, Peter Carey
Promised Lands, Jane Rogers
A Fringe of Leaves,
Patrick White

China and Hong Kong
Wild Swans, Jung Chang
Shanghai Baby, Wei Hui
Kowloon Tong, Paul Theroux

France
Notre Dame de Paris,
Victor Hugo
My Father's Glory, *Jean de
Florette* and *Manon des Sources*,
Marcel Pagnol

India
A Passage to India, EM Forster
Kim, Rudyard Kipling
The God of Small Things,
Arundhati Roy
Midnight's Children,
Salman Rushdie
*The Age of Kali: Indian Travels
and Encounters*,
William Dalrymple

Ireland
Echoes, Maeve Binchy
*Portrait of the Artist as a Young
Man*, James Joyce

Italy
The Talented Mr Ripley,
Patricia Highsmith
The Leopard, Giuseppe Tomasi
di Lampedusa

Japan
Shogun, James Clavell
Memoirs of a Geisha,
Arthur Golden
An Artist of the Floating World,
Kazuo Ishiguro
The Wind-Up Bird Chronicle,
Haurki Murakami

Russia
*Eugene Onegin: A Novel in
Verse*, Alexander Pushkin
Crime and Punishment,
Fyodor Dostoevsky
*Anna Karenina: A Novel in Eight
Parts*, Leo Tolstoy
Doctor Zhivago, Boris Pasternak

Spain
Death in the Afternoon,
Ernest Hemingway
*As I Walked Out One
Midsummer Morning*, Laurie Lee

South America
The Fruit Palace, Charles Nicholl
News of a Kidnapping,
Gabriel Garcia Marquez
Rayuela, Julio Cortazar

US
Absalom, Absalom!,
William Faulkner,
To Kill a Mockingbird,
Harper Lee
Washington Square, Henry James
The Catcher in the Rye,
JD Salinger

D IS FOR DORD

For five years, *Webster's New International Dictionary* famously included an entry for 'dord', a word that does not exist. It was listed between entries for 'Dorcopsis' (a genus of small kangaroo of Papua) and 'doré' (golden in colour), as a noun describing density in the fields of physics and chemistry.

It was a particularly eagle-eyed editor who first aroused suspicions in 1939. He noted that the word was lacking the normal etymological description and searched through the files to track it down. What he found instead was a small card bearing the notation 'D or d, density', which should have been added to the abbreviation section, but had somehow mistakenly turned up in the 'words' pile instead.

'As soon as someone else entered the pronunciation, dord was given the slap on the back that sent breath into its being' explained Philip Babcock Gove, editor-in-chief in 1954. 'Whether the etymologist ever got a chance to stifle it, there is no evidence. It simply has no etymology. Thereafter, only a proofreader had final opportunity at the word, but as the proof passed under his scrutiny he was at the moment not so alert and suspicious as usual'. That's one editorial team who found itself abbreviated to 'D or k, dense'.

YOU ARE HOW YOU READ

The four classes of reader according to Samuel Taylor Coleridge:

• **Sponges,** who absorb all that they read and return it in nearly the same state, only a little dirtied.
• **Sand-glasses,** who retain nothing and are content to get through a book for the sake of getting through the time.
• **Strain-bags,** who retain merely the dregs of what they read.
• **Mogul diamonds,** equally rare and valuable, who profit by what they read, and enable others to profit by it also.

DEEP THOUGHT

In 1997, a group of Cambridge scientists studying the age of the universe found that they had been beaten to the answer by cult novel, *The Hitchhiker's Guide to the Galaxy* (1995). In Douglas Adam's sci-fi classic, an alien race programmes a computer called Deep Thought to study the universe to find the ultimate meaning of life; it returns, seven-and-a-half million years later with the result, 42. It was the same answer that scientists calculated 15 years later after no fewer than three years working on 'The Hubble Constant' (an equation that puts the age of the universe at 23 billion years). That's science fiction for you.

LITERARY LINGOS

Languages of Middle Earth
(*Lord of the Rings* – JRR Tolkien, 1954–1955)

Avarin...........................the language of the Avari elves who were happy
with Middle Earth and refused the summons of the Powers
Doriathrin..the mothertongue of Lúthien
Entish....................................the language of the Onodrim (the Ent race)
Khuzdul..the secret tongue of the Dwarves
Mannish... ....the tongues of men of which Westron is a part
Nandorin..the Silvan Tongue, or Green Elven
Orkish...the language of the Orcs
Quenya..High Elvish
Sindarin...the Noble Tongue, or Grey Elven
Telerin...the language of the Sea-elves
Westron........................the Common Tongue spoken by man and hobbit

ABOUT A B

Some of our best-loved writers prefer a double initial approach, but
what do the AA, the DH or the TS stand for?

WH Auden – *Wystan Hugh*
JM Barrie – *James Matthew*
AS Byatt – *Antonia Susan*
ee cummings – *Edward Estlin*
Edward Estlin has become known as
'the poet who never uses capitals'.
GK Chesterton – *Gilbert Keith*
TS Eliot – *Thomas Stearns*
EM Forster – *Edward Morgan*
AE Housman – *Alfred Edward*
PD James – *Phyllis Dorothy*
DH Lawrence – *David Herbert*
CS Lewis – *Clive Staples*
He actually preferred to be called Jack
JB Priestley – *John Boynton*
JK Rowling – *Joanne Kathleen*
JD Salinger – *Jerome David*
JRR Tolkien – *John Ronald Reuel*
HG Wells – *Herbert George*
PG Wodehouse – *Pelham Grenville*
WS Gilbert – *William Schwenk*
AA Milne – *Alan Alexander*
The illustrator of the Winnie the Pooh *series*
is another double-barreller:
EH Shepard – *Ernest Howard*

FINDING YOUR WAY AROUND

Most libraries use the Dewey Decimal Classification (DCC system) which works to the following classifications:

000–099 *General Works*
199–199 *Philosophy*
200–299 *Religion*
300–399 *Social Studies*
400–499 *Languages*
500–599 *Science*
600–699 *Technology*
700–799 *Fine Arts*
800–899 *Literature*
900–999 *History and Geography*

WRITERS ON READING

In the days of calf love every boy has first tasted the sweetness of literature in two of the best novels ever written, as well as two of the best pieces of good English. One is *Robinson Crusoe* and the other *The Pilgrim's Progress*. Both were written by masters of our tongue, and they remain until this day the purest and most appetising introduction to the book passion. They created two worlds of adventure with minute vivid details and constant surprises – the foot on the sand, for instance, in *Crusoe*, and the valley of the shadow with the hobgoblin in *Pilgrim's Progress* – and one will have a tenderness for these two first loves even until the end. Afterwards one went afield and sometimes got into queer company, not bad but simply a little common. There was an endless series of Red Indian stories in my school-days, wherein trappers could track the enemy by a broken blade of grass, and the enemy escaped by coming down the river under a log, and the price was sixpence each. We used to pass the tuck-shop at school for three days on end in order that we might possess Leaping Deer, the Shawnee Spy. We toadied shamefully to the owner of Bull's Eye Joe, who, we understood, had been the sole protection of a frontier state. Again and again have I tried to find one of those early friends, and in many places have I inquired, but my humble companions have disappeared and left no signs, like country children one played with in holiday times.

Ian Maclaren, *Books and Bookmen*

WHAT'S THAT WORD?

The word 'lethologica' describes the state of not being able to remember the word you want.

UNRAVELLING THE CODE

Handy acronyms for second-hand book purchasing on e-bay...

ARC	Advance reader's copy (usually a paperback edition of a book that is circulated before the trade edition for publicity)
AUTO	Autographed
CTB	Coffee-table book
EXLIB	Ex-library book
F/E	First edition
HB/DJ	Hardback with dust jacket
HIC	Hole in cover
HIST	Historical
MYS	Mystery
SC	Slight crease
NC	No cover
NM	Near mint
OOP	Out of print
PB	Paperback or paperbound
PC	Poor condition
RC	Reader copy (a book in a good condition but with no real investment value)
ROM	Romantic
VGC	Very good condition
VHTF	Very hard to find
WOC	Writing on cover
WYSIWYG	What you see is what you get

And one that should be there:

DBAWOI	Don't believe a word of it

POETIC PUZZLERS

In Dostoevsky's *The Idiot*, who was the idiot?
Answer on page 153.

PAPERBACK SAINTS

St Christopher	bookbinders
St Francis de Sales	authors and journalists
St John of God	booksellers
St John Bosco	editors
St Jerome	librarians
SS David and Celia	poets
SS John of God, Augustine of Hippo	printers

---

34 *Number of storeys in the 'squat grey building' described in the opening
line of Aldous Huxley's* Brave New World *(1932)*

According to Pliny the Elder, Athenian poet **Aeschylus** was killed by a falling tortoise dropped by an eagle in 456 BC.

Italian poet **Dante Alighieri** fell ill and died about an hour after completing *The Divine Comedy* (1321).

Sir Francis Bacon died on 9 April 1626 of suffocation caused by a severe chill, after stuffing a chicken with snow to test his theory of refrigeration.

Lord Byron died in 1824 during a 'blood letting' attempt to cure malarial fever.

William Burroughs accidentally killed his wife when he tried to shoot a glass off her head in Mexico in 1951. He later said that he would never have become a writer but for her death.

British poet **Thomas Chatterton** drank arsenic at the age of 17.

Greek playwright **Euripides** was mauled to death by a pack of wild dogs in 406 BC.

William Faulkner died of a heart attack after falling off a horse in 1962.

American poet **Harold Hart Crane** jumped from a steamboat into the Caribbean Sea in 1932.

Ernest Hemingway shot himself in the mouth in Idaho, in 1961.

In 1983, Hungarian-born British author **Arthur Koestler** committed suicide with his wife when he became terminally ill.

American novelist, **Jack London**, overdosed on morphine in 1916.

In 1593, playwright **Christopher Marlowe**, rumoured to be an Elizabethan secret agent, was stabbed to death in a tavern brawl. He was only 29 years old.

In 1967, English dramatist **Joe Orton** was killed by his hammer-wielding lover Kenneth Halliwell, who subsequently committed suicide.

Sylvia Plath committed suicide by gassing herself in 1963.

George Bernard Shaw died in 1950, aged 94, after he fell from a ladder while pruning an apple tree.

Percy Bysshe Shelley drowned in a sailing accident off the coast of Italy in 1822.

After giving away his entire fortune, **Leo Tolstoy** froze to death in a railway station in 1910.

Tennessee Williams choked to death on a bottle cap at his New York City residence on 24 February 1983.

Virginia Woolf committed suicide by drowning herself in the River Ouse near her home in Rodmell, Sussex in 1941.

**Name the book and author of these famous –
and not-so-famous – opening lines. Answers on page 153.**

1. 1801 – I have just returned from a visit to my landlord – the solitary neighbour that I shall be troubled with.

2. 'Christmas won't be Christmas without any presents,' grumbled Jo, lying on the rug.

3. I am living at the Villa Borghese. There is not a crumb of dirt anywhere nor a chair misplaced. We are alone here and we are dead.

4. The boy with fair hair lowered himself down the last few feet of rock and began to pick his way towards the lagoon.

5. It was love at first sight.

6. What's it going to be then, eh?

7. 'To be born again,' sang Gibreel Farishta tumbling from the heavens, 'first you have to die.'

8. On an exceptionally hot evening early in July a young man came out of the garret in which he lodged in S. Place and walked slowly, as though in hesitation, towards K. bridge.

9. Mr Jones, of the Manor Farm, had locked the hen-house for the night, but was too drunk to remember to shut the popholes.

10. Happy families are all alike; every unhappy family is unhappy in its own way.

11. Someone must have been telling lies about Joseph K., for without having done anything wrong he was arrested one fine morning.

12. There was no possibility of taking a walk that day.

13. As I walked through the wilderness of this world, I lighted on a certain place where was a Den, and laid me down in that place to sleep: and, as I slept, I dreamed a dream.

14. When Mary Lennox was sent to Misselthwaite Manor to live with her uncle everybody said she was the most disagreeable-looking child ever seen.

15. One thing was certain, that the white kitten had nothing to do with it – it was the black kitten's fault entirely.

16. Whether I shall turn out to be the hero of my own life, or whether that station will be held by anybody else, these pages must show.

17. It was a bright cold day in April, and the clocks were striking thirteen.

18. Ours is essentially a tragic age, so we refuse to take it tragically.

36 *Total number of dramatic situations that exist, according to the author Georges Polti in* Thirty-Six Dramatic Situations *(1945)*

THE REWRITE WAS BETTER

Finnegan's Cake
James Joyce charts the story of a publican near Dublin, his wife,
their three children and the pies and pastries they serve.

THE 2003 TOP-SELLING CHILDREN'S BOOKS

1. *Harry Potter and the Order of Phoenix*, JK Rowling
2. *Northern Lights*, Philip Pullman
3. *Harry Potter and the Goblet of Fire*, JK Rowling
4. *Harry Potter and the Prisoner of Azkaban*, JK Rowling
5. *The Lion King*, Disney
6. *The Subtle Knife*, Philip Pullman
7. *The Amber Spyglass*, Philip Pullman
8. *Harry Potter and the Chamber of Secrets*, JK Rowling
9. *Finding Nemo: Book of the Film*, Disney
10. *Harry Potter and the Philosopher's Stone*, JK Rowling

WRITERS ON WRITING

And while the abilities of the nine-hundredth abridger of the History
of England, or of the man who collects and publishes in a volume
some dozen lines of Milton, Pope, and Prior, with a paper from the
Spectator, and a chapter from Sterne, are eulogised by a thousand
pens – there seems almost a general wish of decrying the capacity and
undervaluing the labour of the novelist, and of slighting the perform-
ances which have only genius, wit, and taste to recommend them.

Jane Austen, *Northanger Abbey*

Seasoned quoters take heed, you may not be half as accurate as you think you are...

Commonly: Alas, poor Yorick, I knew him well
Actually: Alas poor Yorick! I knew him, Horatio
Shakespeare, *Hamlet*

Commonly: Accidents will happen
Actually: Accidents will occur
Charles Dickens, *David Copperfield* (1849–1850)

Commonly: Water, water everywhere, but not a drop to drink
 Water, water everywhere, nor e'er a drop to drink
 Water, water everywhere, and not a drop to drink
Actually: Water, water everywhere, nor any drop to drink
Samuel Taylor Coleridge, *Rime of the Ancient Mariner* (1798)

Commonly: A blessing in disguise
Actually: Blessings in disguise
James Hervey, *Reflections on a Flower Garden* (1746)

Commonly: Hell hath no fury like a woman scorned
Actually: Heaven has no rage like love to hatred turned
 Nor hell a fury like a woman scorned
William Congreve, *The Mourning Bride* (1697)

Commonly: Money is the root of all evil
Actually: For the love of money is the root of all evil
The Bible, Timothy 6:10

Commonly: Adding fuel to the fire
Actually: Adding fuel to the flame
John Milton, *Samson Agonistes* (1671)

Commonly: Ask me no questions, and I'll tell you no lies
Actually: Ask me no questions, and I'll tell you no fibs
Oliver Goldsmith, *She Stoops to Conquer* (1774)

Commonly: To gild the lily
Actually: To gild refined gold, to paint the lily
Shakespeare, *King John*

ONCE THEY WERE LIBRARIANS

John Braine • Casanova
Jane Gardam • David Hockney
Sir Ludovic Kennedy • Philip Larkin
August Strindberg • Laurie Taylor
Mao Tse-Tung

WRITERS ON READING

The world of books is the most remarkable creation of man. Nothing else that he builds ever lasts. Monuments fall; nations perish; civilizations grow old and die out; and, after an era of darkness, new races build others. But in the world of books are volumes that have seen this happen again and again, and yet live on, still young, still as fresh as the day they were written, still telling men's hearts of the hearts of men centuries dead.

And even the books that do not last long, penetrate their own times at least, sailing farther than Ulysses even dreamed of, like ships on the seas. It is the author's part to call into being their cargoes and passengers – living thoughts and rich bales of study and jeweled ideas. And as for the publishers, it is they who build the fleet, plan the voyage, and sail on, facing wreck, till they find every possible harbor that will value their burden.

Clarence S Day, *The Story of the Yale University Press*
Told by a Friend

BOOKS THAT BECAME SONGS

1984 – David Bowie
Journey to the Center of the Earth – Rick Wakeman
Rime of the Ancient Mariner – Iron Maiden
Wuthering Heights – Kate Bush
And Then There Were None – Exodus
Romeo and Juliet – Dire Straits
Brave New World – Donovan
Lord of the Flies – Iron Maiden
Blake's Jerusalem – Billy Bragg
For Whom the Bell Tolls – Metallica
Tom Sawyer – Rush
Bell Jar – The Bangles
War of the Worlds – Jeff Wayne
All Quiet on the Western Front – Elton John
On the Road – John Denver
Catcher in the Rye – Clandestine

GHOST DUSTERS

The dust jacket has been hanging around book covers for centuries, but Lewis Carroll can be thanked for its present form. He came up with the very sensible idea of printing the title of *The Hunting of the Snark* (1872) on the spine of the jacket so it could be easily found on a bookshelf.

TEXTUAL HEALING

In July 2002, the National Reading Campaign commissioned a survey of adult reading habits. Here's what they found...

- Ninety-six per cent of readers surveyed had read something in the past week whether books, magazines, newspapers or text messages (which apparently counts as reading).

- Reading material varied according to age: 70% of 16–24-year-olds had read a magazine, compared to 59% of 55–64-year-olds; 33% of 16–24-year-olds had read fiction, compared to 43% of 55–64-year-olds.

- Nearly half the adults had read five books or more in the previous 12 months, with almost one in five claiming to have read 20 books or more.

- A quarter of adults had not read a book at all during the same period, including almost half of males aged between 16 and 24.

- Two out of five adults had read a book after tips from friends; 16% followed recommendations from colleagues.

SORTES VERGILIANAE

There's magic to be found in books and not just in the plot. *Sortes vergilianae* is an ancient method of divining the future based on the 'magic' of Virgil's poetry. Fate is dealt by opening the book at a random page and identifying a line by three throws of the dice. The Roman Emperor Hadrian is said to have consulted the *sortes vergilianae* in an effort to inquire into his future, and many, including St Jerome, believed that Virgil's fourth *Ecologue* (which was written around 41 or 40 BC) predicted the birth of Christ.

It may sound like hocus pocus, but things took a decidedly coincidental twist when the King of England Charles I conjured up his fortune in 1642. Virgil provided the following prophetic line: 'May he be harried in war by audacious tribes and exiled from his own land'. Just seven years later, Oliver Cromwell fulfilled the poet's prophecy by relieving Charles of his head.

40 *Year, in the eleventh century, when the Chinese first printed from movable type. They later discarded the method*

It's every publisher's worst nightmare, but just to prove they don't always get it right, here are our top 10 best-selling literary rejects...

Dubliners, James Joyce
Joyce would not allow any changes to be made in his book of short stories about the darker side of Dublin life. It was rejected by 22 different publishers until finally published in 1914 by Grant Richards. On an earlier print run with Dublin firm Maunsel in 1910, the 1,000 copies were burnt by the publisher as 'offensive, either to the Royal Family or to sexual morality or unpatriotic in its depiction of Dublin'. A furious Joyce quit Ireland in disgust.

Dune, Frank Herbert
Twenty-three publishers rejected this work of science fiction as 'too slow' and 'too long'. It has since become the number one science fiction tale of all time with sales in the tens of millions.

M*A*S*H, Richard Hooker
The novel took seven years to write and 21 rejections until it was finally published by Morrow.

Jonathan Livingstone Seagull, Richard Bach
Refused as 'unpromising' by 18 publishers, the first print run sold over seven million copies in the US alone.

Lorna Doone, RD Blackmore
Eighteen rejections before it was finally printed.

No Thanks, ee cummings
Thirteen publishers rejected the manuscript until it was finally published by his mother. Under the dedication, cummings wrote 'WITH NO THANKS TO...' and proceeded to list the publishers who had turned it down.

Anne Frank: The Diary of a Young Girl, Anne Frank
This extraordinary work was turned down 11 times as 'unsatisfactory' although 'promising' before finally making it to print in 1952.

The Tale of Peter Rabbit, Beatrix Potter
After rejections from at least six publishing houses, Potter used her savings to privately publish the book in 1901. She found a publisher in 1902 and by the end of 1903, had sold 50,000 copies.

Life of Pi, Yann Martel
At least five London publishers rejected this Booker Prize-winner until the small Edinburgh publisher Canongate picked up the magical tale.

Harry Potter and the Philosopher's Stone, JK Rowling
After four rejections, Bloomsbury agreed to purchase Rowling's manuscript, and the rest is history.

Britain's best-loved books as voted in the 2003 BBC Big Read...

1. *The Lord of the Rings*, JRR Tolkien
2. *Pride and Prejudice*, Jane Austen
3. *His Dark Materials*, Philip Pullman
4. *The Hitchhiker's Guide to the Galaxy*, Douglas Adams
5. *Harry Potter and the Goblet of Fire*, JK Rowling
6. *To Kill a Mockingbird*, Harper Lee
7. *Winnie the Pooh*, AA Milne
8. *1984*, George Orwell
9. *The Lion, the Witch and the Wardrobe*, CS Lewis
10. *Jane Eyre*, Charlotte Brontë
11. *Catch-22*, Joseph Heller
12. *Wuthering Heights*, Emily Brontë
13. *Birdsong*, Sebastian Faulks
14. *Rebecca*, Daphne du Maurier
15. *The Catcher in the Rye*, JD Salinger
16. *The Wind in the Willows*, Kenneth Grahame
17. *Great Expectations*, Charles Dickens
18. *Little Women*, Louisa May Alcott
19. *Captain Corelli's Mandolin*, Louis de Bernières
20. *War and Peace*, Leo Tolstoy
21. *Gone with the Wind*, Margaret Mitchell

Not only did 500,000 people vote for their favourite books, but figures released shortly after the poll showed that sales of the top 21 books had increased by a massive 524%, with library lending increasing by 56% in the same period. DVD and videos did even better; sales of movie versions of 15 books of the books jumped by 1,500%. The Hollywood version of *Captain Corelli's Mandolin* proved one of the biggest winners with a 1,553% rise compared to the 155% increase recorded for the novel.

WRITERS ON WRITING

> There is no frigate like a book
> To take us lands away,
> Nor any coursers like a page
> Of prancing poetry.
> This traverse may the poorest take
> Without oppress of toll;
> How frugal is the chariot
> That bears a human soul!

Emily Dickinson, *A Book*

Total number of fellowship grants (worth $840,000) awarded in 2004 to authors of prose in the US by the National Endowment for the Arts

Reader, I carried him.

LITERARY GAMES AND LINGOS

The Glass Bead Game (Hermann Hesse, 1943)

Played out in the futuristic post-Holocaust land of Castalia, Hesse's Glass Bead Game – an ancient symbolic language game – demands a mastery of music, mathematics, philosophy and logic if it is to be understood. Presided over by the Magister Ludi, it is used to interpret and predict social developments and its dictates are treated with the gravest reverence in Castalia and beyond.

Undaunted by the fact that Hesse does not provide a comprehensive list of symbols or rules of play for his hypothetical language, several societies have sprung up since the book's publication determined to play the game and use their readings for good. We can only wish them luck!

PRINT-RUN RECORD

Book five of the Harry Potter series holds the record for the largest print run in history. Thirteen million hardback copies of *Harry Potter and Order of the Phoenix* were printed to meet the huge demand generated for its release, which saw 875,000 advance orders taken on Amazon.com alone. *Harry Potter and the Goblet of Fire* (book four) holds the record for the most advance orders; a colossal 5.3 million copies (that's around 40 times as many as the average bestseller) were ordered and prepaid worldwide before its release.

POETIC PUZZLERS

**Four writers joined by one cinematic theme.
Name the link and the films...**

JG Ballard • Robert Harling
Stephen King • Irvine Welsh
Answer on page 153.

LITERARY RECLUSES

Probably the literary world's most famous recluse, **JD Salinger** went into hiding in the hills of New Hampshire after his debut novel *The Catcher in the Rye* (1951) became a massive success.

Nobel Laureate **JM Coetzee** didn't show up to collect either of his Booker Prizes.

Don DeLillo rarely gives readings and keeps interviews to a minimum. He once handed over a piece of paper inscribed with the words: 'I don't want to talk about it,' so he wouldn't even have to voice his answer.

Loner **John Fowles**, author of *The French Lieutenant's Woman,* despises literary pomp and is notoriously uneasy around other writers who he considers 'vain' and self-serving. He can be found in self-imposed exile in one of the wildest spots of the South Coast.

Thomas Harris courteously refuses all enquiries from journalists with the words: 'I really can't start giving interviews now.' He also rejects all editorial suggestions on his writing.

Thomas Pynchon, author of *Gravity's Rainbow* and *V*, is so publicity-shy he once dived out of an apartment window in Mexico City to escape a photographer. He ran away into the mountains, where he hid long enough to grow a moustache and gain the local nickname 'Pancho Villa'. According to one legend, he is actually JD Salinger.

LITERARY PRIZES

The British Poet Laureate fulfils a variety of functions: they are the realm's official poet (and accepted as such into the royal household) with tasks that include writing verses for court and national occasions. Once chosen by the British reigning monarch from a list of nominees compiled by the Prime Minister, the post is awarded and accepted for life.

The ceremony takes its name from the Latin *laureatus* ('crowned with laurel') which derives from the ancient Roman tradition of honouring excellence in poetic achievement.

So far there have been 19 Poets Laureate. The first British Poet Laureate was Edmund Spenser. He fulfilled the role from 1591 to his death in 1599 despite the fact that the first folio edition of *The Faerie Queene* wasn't published until 10 years after his death.

The current Poet Laureate is Andrew Motion. He accepted the role in 1998 and has been serving ever since.

The longest-serving Poet Laureate was Alfred Lord Tennyson. He held the post for 42 years from 1850 until his death in 1892.

The shortest-serving Poets Laureate were Thomas Shadwell (1642–1692) and Nicholas Rowe (1674–1718), both of whom quit their posts after only three years.

The oldest Poet Laureate was John Masefield (1885–1977). He was 92 when he ended his 37-year reign. The oldest to accept the post was William Wordsworth: he picked up the title at the age of 73.

The youngest was Laurence Eusden, who became Poet Laureate at the tender age of 30.

John Dryden was the only Poet Laureate to be dismissed from the post. He was sacked for not taking an oath of allegiance to William III.

Quentin Blake became the first Children's Laureate in 1999. Ann Fine replaced him in May 2001.

ONE AND A HALF FOOT

Derived from the Latin '*sesquipedalis*' (literally, a foot-and-a-half long), the word 'sesquipedalian' is used to describe the size or the use of long words. It was passed down by the Roman poet Horace who mentions *sesquipedalia verba*, or 'foot-and-a-half-long words', in *Ars poetica* ('the art of poetry'). Fittingly, the word itself provides some of the longest sesquipdalians: writers who use long words are described as sesquipedalianists; their style of writing is sesquipedalianism, the habit of using them is sesquipedality, and a hyperpolysyllabicsesquipedalianist is someone who takes pride in their use of really long words.

Amount, in thousands of dollars, paid at a charity auction for 93 words 45
written by JK Rowling that hinted at the plot of the fifth Harry Potter book

Divine punishment for the deceased in Dante's *The Divine Comedy*
Nine hellish circles to think about while you still can...

Purgatory: Those not evil enough to make it to hell proper are condemned to linger here. Guilty of having lived neutral uncommitted lives, these poor souls are repeatedly stung by insects.

1 Populated by virtuous pagans and unbaptised infants, hell's first circle (otherwise known as Limbo) is the circle of choice for the discerning sinner. Although condemned to perpetual melancholy, you can at least be sure of good conversation, being blessed with Homer, Socrates and Plato for company.

2: It's in this circle that you'll face judgement before being sent to the Elysian Fields or everlasting torment. The Carnal will remain here alongside Dido, Cleopatra, Helen of Troy and Paris. Be warned however: the punishment here – being blown for ever by stormy winds – could render any kind of chit-chat impossible.

3: You've just stumbled into the arena of the Gluttons. Guarded by Cerberus, lying prostrate in mud and besieged by snow, hail and filthy water, you might question whether that extra helping was a wise decision after all.

4: Avaricious? Prodigal? Change your ways or an eternity of useless labour awaits you here.

5: Reserved for the Angry and the Sullen, in the fifth circle 'an eye for an eye' rules supreme. If your life was spent in anger, you are at risk of attack from your fellow internees. As consolation, hitting back is encouraged. For the sullen, don't expect any let-up – you'll be submerged in the Styx, your self-pitying sighs gently rippling the water.

6: If you're claustrophobic, pray you don't end up here. Set aside for Heretics, this circle's gratuitous punishment involves confinement in a burning tomb.

7: For the Violent (against man and God) the tortures of the seventh circle range from being dunked in hot blood to being stretched out on hot sand. Sodomites are also imprisoned here and forced to run for penance under fiery rain.

8: Panders, Seducers, Hypocrites and other Shysters languish here. They are whipped by devils, covered with filth, or have their heads turned backwards. Ulysses is your famous fellow sinner.

9: Hell's deepest circle, set aside for those who have acted treacherously towards their family or country, or who have murdered a guest. Packed with celebrities (including Lucifer himself, Brutus and Judas). If you were wicked enough to end up here, torture by ice awaits you – all this, of course, while suffering Lucifer's freezing blasts of hatred.

LITERARY LATIN

acte est fabula – the play is finished
ars gratia artis – art for art's sake
ex libris – from the library of
index librorum prohibitorum – list of forbidden books
lector benevole – kind reader
literati – men of letters
magnum opus – the greatest piece of work (of an artist)
ps (post scriptum) – written later
theatrum mundi – the theatre of the world
ubi supra – where (cited) above
v.l. (varia lecto) – variant reading

QUOTE UNQUOTE

Every journalist has a novel in him,
which is an excellent place for it.
J Russel Lynes, US author and critic

EKERS AND GUSHERS

Flaubert was an 'eker'. Intent on finding the right word ('le mot juste'), he rarely squeezed out more than a paragraph a day.

Samuel Johnson wrote *Rasselas* in one week to raise money to pay for his mother's funeral. He sold it to a publisher for £100 without even reading it over once.

Louisa May Alcott authored *Little Women* in two and a half months. The resulting sales pulled her out of poverty.

Dame Barbara Cartland was one of the world's most gushing authors; even in her 80s, she was writing an average of 23 books a year. In her 77-year career, she managed to churn out over 700 books.

Enid Blyton was without doubt the most prolific children's writer of the twentieth century. By the time of her death in 1968, she had also become the most published author of all time with over 700 books and 10,000 short stories to her name.

Harold St John Hamilton (Frank Richards) wins the award for the most words ever written. The author who created *Billy Bunter* put around 75 million to paper.

Taking the crown from Enid Blyton, Brazilian **Jose Carlos Ryoki di Alpoim Inoiue** became the most prolific novelist of all time when he published 1,058 novels between 1986 and 1996 – that's more than 105 a year.

CREATIVE COCK-UPS

Long-winded writer Marcel Proust received a rejection letter from French publishing house Fasquelle with the words: 'My dear fellow, I may be dead from the neck up, but rack my brains as I may, I can't see why a chap should need thirty pages to describe how he turns over in bed before going to sleep.' When the novel, *Remembrance of Things Past*, was subsequently published, this passage hadn't been cut.

WHAT'S IN A NAME?

William Faulkner's name is actually spelled 'Falkner'. The printer who set up his name for his first book misspelt it (adding the 'u') and Faulkner decided to live with the new name rather than bother to correct his editor.

TOP TEN LITERARY VILLAINS

Good has been pitted against evil since the earliest literary texts; here are some of the best bad boys (and machines)...

Big Brother – The all-seeing dictator of Oceania in George Orwell's *1984*

Captain Ahab – The deranged captain intent on killing the white whale in Herman Melville's *Moby-Dick*

Captain Hook – Peter Pan's hooked nemesis from JM Barrie's *Peter Pan and Wendy*

Grendel – The monstrous demon from the old English epic *Beowulf*

Iago – The treacherous back-stabber in Shakespeare's *Othello*

Jack – William Golding's cruel and power-hungry youth leader in *The Lord of the Flies*

Mr Kurtz – The tortured villain of Joseph Conrad's novel *Heart of Darkness*

Satan – The ruler of hell in John Milton's *Paradise Lost* and Dante's *The Divine Comedy*

Sauron – The dark lord in JRR Tolkien's *The Lord of the Rings*

Scrooge, Ebenezer – The villain turned hero in Charles Dickens' *A Christmas Carol*

QUOTE UNQUOTE

In America only the successful writer is important, in France all writers are important, in England no writer is important, and in Australia you have to explain what a writer is.
Geoffrey Cottrell, humorist

AN ENCYCLOPEDIC HISTORY

The term 'encyclopedia' comes from the Greek *enkyklios paideia*, which translates as 'a circle of learning'.

The first attempt at an encyclopedia was made more than 2,000 years ago, but the name encyclopedia was not used for such works until the sixteenth century.

Greek philosopher Aristotle is known as the 'father of encyclopedias' because of his written attempts to summarise all existing knowledge. But the first encyclopedia is said to have been compiled in the fourth century BC by Greek philosopher Speusippus, a student of Plato.

Natural History (c. 77 AD) by the Roman scholar Pliny the Elder is the oldest complete encyclopedia still in existence. It has 37 volumes and remained popular for almost 1,500 years.

Etymologies, or Origins (623 AD) was compiled by Spanish scholar Saint Isidore of Seville and included subjects such as medicine, animals, the earth, grammar, war and games.

The largest encyclopedia was created in the sixteenth century by the Chinese. The *Yung Lo Ta Tien* was compiled by over 5,000 writers and bound in more than 11,000 volumes.

Encyclopedias were for centuries arranged so that they began with God and angels. English philosopher and statesman Francis Bacon was the first to organise a proper structure for his *The Great Reconstruction* (1620), but he never completed the project.

The alphabetical and subject arrangement of encyclopedias began during the eighteenth century. French philosopher and critic Pierre Bayle's two-volume *Historical and Critical Dictionary* (1697) was famed for its simplicity and clarity of style.

The 28-volume *Encyclopédie* (1751–1772) compiled by French philosopher and dramatist Denis Diderot employed a team of mathematicians, philosophers and academics and claimed 'to exhibit as far as possible the order and system of human knowledge, and contain the fundamental principles and essential details of every science and art, whether liberal or mechanical'.

Encyclopedia Britannica was first published in 100 parts from 1768 to 1771 before being bound into three volumes.

The first CD-ROM encyclopedia was produced in 1985, and in 1993 Microsoft released *Encarta Encyclopedia*, the first to have no accompanying books.

Literary collaborations that could have been:

Gone with the Wind in the Willows (Mitchell/Grahame)
Mole, Ratty and Badger struggle to defend their beloved riverside plantation from being ravaged during the Civil War. Toad, however, doesn't give a damn.

The Dice Man who Mistook his Wife for a Hat (Rhinehart/Sacks)
A psychiatrist treats his seriously disturbed patients based on the random dictates of a die with hilarious and harrowing results.

Brave New World According to Garp (Huxley/Irving)
The bastard son of Jenny Field consumes daily grams of soma to fight his terminal depression.

The Quiet American Psycho (Greene/Easton Ellis)
High-flying, murderous and psychopathic Genesis fan flies to Vietnam to take on a well-intentioned mission of political enlightenment.

On the Road to Welville (Kerouac/Coraghessan)
Colonic irrigation for motorcyclists.

Band of Brothers Karamazov (Ambrose/Dostoevsky)
Inexplicably fighting for the US Army in World War Two, the Karamazov brothers have little time to mull over the other's moral stance and consequently get on fabulously.

Quiet Flows the Don Quixote (Sholokhov/Cervantes)
Sholokhov seeks to correct the unfavorable image of the Don Cossacks by following the adventures of Don Quixote of La Mancha and his faithful squire, Sancho Panza, as they travel through twentieth-century Russia.

Stupid White Men are from Mars, Women are from Venus (Moore/Gray)
Intolerable self-help guide rendered even more intolerable by the addition of self-congratulatory political posturing.

Watership Down and Out in Paris and London Adams/Orwell)
Evicted from their riverside burrows, Bigwig and Bluebell try their luck tramping about the two capital cities.

BOOK RECORDS

The record for unsupported book balancing goes to John Evans of Sheffield. In 1998, he balanced no fewer than 62 identical books on his head – that's a book tower 185.4cm (73in) in height.

Skating for Godot
Trapped in an absurd wait for the arrival of Godot, Vladimir and Esthergon quarrel, make up, contemplate suicide, try to sleep, eat a carrot and partake in a spot of ice-skating.

THE POWER OF THREE

Three Blind Mice – Agatha Christie (1950)
The Three Clerks – Anthony Trollope (1858)
Three Guineas – Virginia Woolf (1931)
Three Hostages – John Buchan (1924)
Three Men in a Boat – Jerome K Jerome (1889)
Three Men on the Bummel – Jerome K Jerome (1900)
(Also known as *Three Men on Wheels*)
The Three Musketeers – Alexandre Dumas (1844)
The Three Sisters – Anton Chekhov (1901)

QUOTE UNQUOTE

It took me 15 years to discover I had no talent for writing, but I couldn't give it up because by that time I was too famous.
Robert Benchley, US author

Number of languages that novels by Sidney Sheldon have been translated 51 into. He is the world's most translated novelist

THE BIG BANG

In 2002, gunpowder that may have been used by Guy Fawkes in his attempt to blow up the Houses of Parliament was discovered in the basement of the British Library. It was unearthed in an old stationery box marked with a photograph of the Houses of Parliament (surely a dead giveaway?) that had been given to the library in 1995 as part of the John Evelyn Collection. But both it – and the letter inside in John Evelyn's handwriting suggesting the gunpowder belonged to Guy Fawkes – were only revealed when the collection was being catalogued over seven years later. Talk about sitting on a time bomb.

WHO BORROWED WHAT AND WHEN

Each year Public Lending Right releases data which reveals the most borrowed books and authors in the nation's libraries. Here are the top picks from July 2002 to June 2003...

1. *The Summons*, John Grisham (2002)
2. *Jinnie*, Josephine Cox (2002)
3. *The Woman Who Left*, Josephine Cox (2001)
4. *Harry Potter and the Chamber of Secrets*, JK Rowling (1999)
5. *Looking Back*, Josephine Cox (2000)
6. *Harry Potter and the Prisoner of Azkaban*, JK Rowling (2000)
7. *Let It Shine*, Josephine Cox (2001)
8. *The Story of Tracy Beaker*, Jacqueline Wilson (1992)
9. *Lizzie Zipmouth*, Jacqueline Wilson (2000)
10. *Girl from the South*, Joanna Trollope (2002)
11. *The Kiss*, Danielle Steel (2001)
12. *Quentin's*, Maeve Binchy (2002)
13. *The Silent Lady*, Catherine Cookson (2001)
14. *The Cottage*, Danielle Steel (2002)
15. *Scarlet Feather*, Maeve Binchy (2002)

FLYING HIGH

Toy company Mattel offered children a less than innocent experience in 2001 when they launched the Harry Potter Nimbus 2000. A toy replica of the broomstick Harry Potter uses in the film version of *Harry Potter and the Philosopher's Stone*, the Nimbus 2000 comes complete with grooved stick, handle for easy riding, magical swooping and wooshing sounds and, to enhance the excitement, the vibrating effects that have made it a top-seller in the nation's sex shops. It seems JK Rowling had a point when she said the Harry Potter series wasn't just for children.

52 *Year, in the twentieth century, when* Uncle Tom's Cabin *was published, the first US novel to sell one million copies*

Nineteenth-century American satirist Ambrose Bierce offers his sardonic views on the writing habit...

BLANK-VERSE, *n.* Unrhymed iambic pentameters – the most difficult kind of English verse to write acceptably; a kind, therefore, much affected by those who cannot acceptably write any kind.

DICTIONARY, *n.* A malevolent literary device for cramping the growth of a language and making it hard and inelastic. This dictionary, however, is a most useful work.

DRAMATIST, *n.* One who adapts plays from the French.

ELEGY, *n.* A composition in verse, in which, without employing any of the methods of humor, the writer aims to produce in the reader's mind the dampest kind of dejection. The most famous English example begins somewhat like this:

> The cur foretells the knell of parting day;
> The loafing herd winds slowly o'er the lea;
> The wise man homeward plods; I only stay
> To fiddle-faddle in a minor key.

GRAMMAR, *n.* A system of pitfalls thoughtfully prepared for the feet for the self-made man, along the path by which he advances to distinction.

NIHILIST, *n.* A Russian who denies the existence of anything but Tolstoy. The leader of the school is Tolstoy.

NOVEL, *n.* A short story padded. A species of composition bearing the same relation to literature that the panorama bears to art. As it is too long to be read at a sitting the impressions made by its successive parts are successively effaced, as in the panorama. Unity, totality of effect, is impossible; for besides the few pages last read all that is carried in mind is the mere plot of what has gone before. To the romance the novel is what photography is to painting. Its distinguishing principle, probability, corresponds to the literal actuality of the photograph and puts it distinctly into the category of reporting; whereas the free wing of the romancer enables him to mount to such altitudes of imagination as he may be fitted to attain; and the first three essentials of the literary art are imagination, imagination and imagination. The art of writing novels, such as it was, is long dead everywhere except in Russia, where it is new. Peace to its ashes -- some of which have a large sale.

PLAGIARIZE, *v.* To take the thought or style of another writer whom one has never, never read.

PROOF-READER, *n.* A malefactor who atones for making your writing nonsense by permitting the compositor to make it unintelligible.

QUOTATION, *n.* The act of repeating erroneously the words of another. The words erroneously repeated.

READING, *n.* The general body of what one reads. In our country it consists, as a rule, of Indiana novels, short stories in 'dialect' and humor in slang.

REALISM, *n.* The art of depicting nature as it is seen by toads. The charm suffusing a landscape painted by a mole, or a story written by a measuring-worm.

RIME, *n.* Agreeing sounds in the terminals of verse, mostly bad. The verses themselves, as distinguished from prose, mostly dull. Usually (and wickedly) spelled 'rhyme'.

ROMANCE, *n.* Fiction that owes no allegiance to the God of Things as They Are. In the novel the writer's thought is tethered to probability, as a domestic horse to the hitching-post, but in romance it ranges at will over the entire region of the imagination – free, lawless, immune to bit and rein.

STORY, *n.* A narrative, commonly untrue.

WITTICISM, *n.* A sharp and clever remark, usually quoted, and seldom noted; what the Philistine is pleased to call a 'joke'.

THE TAMING OF THE LEWD

Victorian to the core, English editor Reverend Thomas Bowdler attacked his editions of Shakespeare, Chaucer and Gibbons with a prudish red pen believing that nothing 'can afford an excuse for profanity or obscenity; and if these could be obliterated, the transcendent genius of the poet would undoubtedly shine with more unclouded lustre'. The result – the severe cutting of everything he considered to be indecent or indelicate – became known as 'bowdlerising'. Bowdler also 'cleaned up' Tennyson's *The Wreck of the Hesperus*, substituting such offensive terms as 'bull' with the explanation 'gentleman cow'.

NO PLACE LIKE UNDER THE TOME

He wasn't the first to sleep at his library desk, but he was certainly the first to move in. In 2004, a homeless New York student said he slept for seven months in a university library without being caught because he couldn't afford his housing costs on top of his tuition fees. The underground life of Steve Stanzak in the Bobst Library on New York's Washington Square – including all the gory details about where he washed and kept his clothes and books (surely on the shelves) – can be read in all its glory on www.homelessatnyu.com.

THE TITLE, THE TITLE AND NOTHING BUT THE FULL TITLE

The full titles of books often better known by their shortened forms

The Fortunes and Misfortunes of the Famous Moll Flanders,
Daniel Defoe (1722)

The History of Tom Jones, a Foundling,
Henry Fielding (1749)

The Life and Opinions of Tristram Shandy,
Lawrence Sterne (1759–1767)

The Life and Strange and Surprising Adventures of Robinson Crusoe,
Daniel Defoe (1719)

The Posthumous Papers of the Pickwick Club,
Charles Dickens (1837)

The Strange Case of Dr Jekyll and Mr Hyde,
Robert Louis Stevenson (1886)

Three Men in a Boat (To say Nothing of the Dog),
Jerome K Jerome (1889)

Through the Looking Glass ...and what Alice Found There,
Lewis Carroll (1871)

The Alchemist: A Fable About Following Your Dream,
Paulo Coelho (1995)

WRITERS ON READING

Some read for style, and some for argument: one has little care about the sentiment, he observes only how it is expressed; another regards not the conclusion, but is diligent to mark how it is inferred; they read for other purposes than the attainment of practical knowledge; and are no more likely to grow wise by an examination of a treatise of moral prudence, than an architect to inflame his devotion by considering attentively the proportions of a temple.

Some read that they may embellish their conversation, or shine in dispute; some that they may not be detected in ignorance, or want the reputation of literary accomplishments: but the most general and prevalent reason of study is the impossibility of finding another amusement equally cheap or constant, equally independent on the hour or the weather. He that wants money to follow the chase of pleasure through her yearly circuit, and is left at home when the gay world rolls to Bath or Tunbridge; he whose gout compels him to hear from his chamber the rattle of chariots transporting happier beings to plays and assemblies, will be forced to seek in books a refuge from himself.

Samuel Johnson, *Adventurer* #137 (1754)

Number of languages into which Anne Frank: The Diary of a Young Girl *(1952)* 55
has been translated

To believe or not to believe? Shakespeare has taken a beating when it comes to the question of his authorship; here are some of the leading theories against him…

- Baconians believe it was Francis Bacon who actually wrote the plays. This popular nineteenth-century theory hinges on Bacon's legal experience and proximity to the court, which is said to better explain their composition, and the use of the word 'honorificabilitudinitatibus' (the writer's longest word) in *Love's Labour's Lost*.

- Marlovians attribute authorship to Christopher Marlowe. They believe the playwright faked his own death in 1593 before penning the plays under the *nom de plume* of Shakespeare.

- Some scholars claim Queen Elizabeth I was responsible, while others believe it was her illegitimate son. Both camps believe that Shakespeare's name was used as means to escape 'vulgar fame'.

- Scholars in Oxford attribute Shakespeare's comedies to Edward de Vere, the seventeenth Earl of Oxford. It is a view heartily espoused by the Earl's descendants who refer to Shakespeare, rather disdainfully, as 'that Stratford man'.

- In a 1989 Iranian radio broadcast, Colonel Gaddafi proposed another far-fetched theory. He claimed that Shakespeare had plagiarised his Euro-centered tragedies and comedies from Arab folktales, and also made the outlandish assertion that Shakespeare (or should that be 'Sheik Speare' was himself of Arab origin).

- Shakespeare's sister wrote the plays (behind every successful man…)

- The most prevalent theory, however, attributes Shakespeare's works to a 'committee' of writers and editors on the premise that no one man is capable of writing such a rich and varied body of work.

In the early 1990s, undergraduates in Claremont College, California, used a computer programme to analyse the word usage in the Bard's plays and poems to see whether it matched the style of 58 alternative candidates. Sir Walter Raleigh came the closest with a pitiful 2% match, Edward de Vere was ranked seventh, and Bacon and Marlowe were miles out with a less than 1% match each. When it came to his poetry, however, all three ranked better than Shakespeare himself – the Bard coming in as the eleventh most probable author of the sonnets.

WRITERS ON WRITING

It was upon the whole a very distinguished party, for independent-
ly of the lesser theatrical lights who clustered on this occasion
round Mr Snittle Timberry, there was a literary gentleman present
who had dramatised in his time two hundred and forty-seven
novels as fast as they had come out – some of them faster than they
had come out – and who WAS a literary gentleman in consequence.
Charles Dickens, *The Life and Adventures of Nicholas Nickleby*

POETIC PUZZLERS

How many novels did the Brontë sisters write?
Answer on page 153.

THE REAL EPICS

- The world's longest nonfiction work is *The Yongle Dadian*, a
  10,000-volume encyclopaedia produced by 5,000 scholars
  during the Ming Dynasty in China 500 years ago.

- The 2,000-year-old *Mahabharata*, the 'Great Epic of India', could
  well be the world's largest book in poetic form. It began at 24,000
  couplets and has gradually expanded to just over 100,000.

- The longest novel is Marcel Proust's *Remembrance of Things
  Past*. The 13-volume work contains a total of 9,609,000
  characters, with each letter and space counting as one character.

- The world's largest book is known to be *The Golden Book of
  Cleveland*. It measures five feet by seven feet, contains 6,000
  pages for signatures and weighs about two and a half tonnes.

- The longest spoken epic in the world is the Tibetan story *King
  Gesser*. The 20-million-word tale takes six hours to recite.

- The longest poem was written by prolific Indian Poet Nikhil
  Parekh. *Only as Life* measures a herculean 1,470 lines, 1,100
  stanzas and 7,900 words.

- The longest dictionary is the *Oxford Dictionary of National
  Biography*, a 60,000-page compilation of 60 volumes that
  would take up a full 11 feet on your bookshelf.

QUOTE UNQUOTE

*Fiction is like a spider's web, attached ever so lightly perhaps, but
still attached to life at all four corners.*
Virginia Woolf, novelist

Number of manuscripts, in millions, housed in the US Library of Congress 57

Over the years Shakespeare has proved a rich resource for titles of books and plays. But it's not only his phrases, titles or characters that have been pinched off the page; even his stage directions have been resurrected in title form...

'Another part of the forest' (*As You Like It*, Act III, scene v)
Another Part of the Forest, Lillian Hellman (1948)
In Another Part of the Forest: An Anthology of Gay Short Fiction,
Alberto Manguel and Craig Stephenson (1994)

'Enter a Gentlewoman' (*The Tragedy of Coriolanus*, Act I, scene iii)
Enter a Gentlewoman, Sara Woods (1982)

'Alarum. Excursion' (*King Henry VI*, Act IV, scene iv)
Alarum and Excursion, Virginia Perdue (1976)
Alarums and Excursions, James Agate (2001)

'Enter Three Witches' (*Macbeth*, Act I, scene i)
Enter Three Witches, Paul McGuire (1985)
Enter Three Witches, Kate Gilmore (1992)

'Exeunt Murderers' (*Macbeth*, Act III, scene i)
Exeunt Murderers: The Best Mystery Stories of Anthony Boucher,
Anthony Boucher (1983)

'Another part of the field' (*Macbeth*, Act V, scene vii)
*Another Part of the Field: Philadelphia's American Revolution,
1777–78*, Robert I Alotta (1991)

'Another part of the wood' (*A Midsummer's Night's Dream*,
Act II, scene ii)
Another Part of the Wood: A Self Portrait, Kenneth Clark (1975)
Another Part of the Wood, Beryl Bainbridge (2004)

'Bohemia. The sea-coast' (*The Winter's Tale*, Act III, scene iii)
The Seacoast of Bohemia, Franklin D Walker (1973)
The Seacoast of Bohemia, Nicholas Freeling (1995)

'Before Prospero's cell' (*The Tempest*, Act IV, scene i)
*Prospero's Cell: A Guide to the Landscape and Manners of the
Island of Corcyra*, Lawrence Durrell (1996)

'The Queen's closet' (*Hamlet*, Act III, scene iv)
Secrets of the Queen's Closet, Tom Isitt (1988)

WHAT'S A 'BOOK'?

Stating the obvious it may be, but UNESCO certainly felt the book needed to be defined in 1950 when they qualified it as 'a non-periodical literary publication containing 49 or more pages, not counting the covers'. The word itself derives from the Latin 'liber', which originally described the thin peel found between the bark and the wood that was used to jot down notes before the era of parchment. The English word comes from 'bog', the Danish for book, which itself is derived from the name of their bark of choice, birch.

WRITERS ON READING

Bessie asked if I would have a book: the word BOOK acted as a transient stimulus, and I begged her to fetch *Gulliver's Travels* from the library. This book I had again and again perused with delight. I considered it a narrative of facts, and discovered in it a vein of interest deeper than what I found in fairy tales: for as to the elves, having sought them in vain among foxglove leaves and bells, under mushrooms and beneath the ground-ivy mantling old wall-nooks, I had at length made up my mind to the sad truth, that they were all gone out of England to some savage country where the woods were wilder and thicker, and the population more scant; whereas, Lilliput and Brobdignag being, in my creed, solid parts of the earth's surface, I doubted not that I might one day, by taking a long voyage, see with my own eyes the little fields, houses, and trees, the diminutive people, the tiny cows, sheep, and birds of the one realm; and the corn-fields forest-high, the mighty mastiffs, the monster cats, the tower-like men and women, of the other. Yet, when this cherished volume was now placed in my hand – when I turned over its leaves, and sought in its marvellous pictures the charm I had, till now, never failed to find – all was eerie and dreary; the giants were gaunt goblins, the pigmies malevolent and fearful imps, Gulliver a most desolate wanderer in most dread and dangerous regions. I closed the book, which I dared no longer peruse, and put it on the table, beside the untasted tart.

Charlotte Brontë, *Jane Eyre*

QUOTE UNQUOTE

A truly great book should be read in youth, again in maturity and once more in old age, as a fine building should be seen by morning light, at noon and by moonlight.
Robertson Davies, Canadian author

THE OPRAH EFFECT

Every time Oprah Winfrey features a new book in her TV-show book club, it rises in the bestseller list. The club had already created 48 bestsellers when it was temporarily disbanded in 2002, and since its relaunch in 2003 with a new focus on classics, books such as *East of Eden* by John Steinbeck, and *Anna Karenina* by Leo Tolstoy have shot to the top of bestseller lists in the US. The Pevear-Volokhonsky translation of *Anna Karenina*, for example, went straight to number one on the *New York Times* book list within one week of being featured on Oprah's show. Penguin has already returned to press twice to cater for the growing demand, which has seen 900,000 copies sold since May 2004, compared to the 60,000 copies which had been bought since the book's US release in 2001. Who says television kills reading?

TOP BIDDERS

Exceptional prices paid at Christie's...

World Auction Record for a seventeenth century book – US$6,166,000
(New York, 2001) First folio edition of *Comedies, Tragedies & Histories,* William Shakespeare (1623)

World Auction Record for a manuscript – US$30,802,500
(New York, 1994) *Codex Hammer*, Leonardo da Vinci

World Auction Record for an illuminated manuscript – £8,580,000
(London, 1999) *Book of Hours, The Rothschild Prayer Book* (1505)

World Auction Record for any printed book – US$8,802,500
(New York, 2000) *The Birds of America*, from *Original Drawings*, John James Audubon

World Auction Record for an incunable – £4,621,500
(London, 1998) *The Canterbury Tales*, Geoffrey Chaucer (1476 or 1477). The book was one of the first major works printed in England by William Caxton, in 1477.

World Auction Record for a Bible – US$5,390,000
(New York, 1987) *The Gutenberg Bible*

World Auction Record for a medical book – US$1,652,500
(New York, 1998) Charles V's coloured copy of *De humani corporis fabrica libri septem*, Andreas Vesalius (1543)

World Auction Record for a children's book – US$1,542,500
(New York, 1998) Suppressed first edition of *Alice's Adventures in Wonderland*, Lewis Carroll (1865)

In 2004, World Book Day commissioned a survey of reading habits by profession. Here's what they found...

- Accountants are the biggest readers, spending an average of five hours and 15 minutes a week on their preferred authors (Jane Austen and JRR Tolkien). They tend to do most of their reading during the commute to work.

- Secretaries came second with just under five hours a week. They also like Jane Austen, but tend to do most of their reading in bed.

- Politicians came a close third (also just under five hours). Half preferred histories while 47% opted for biographies – Betty Boothroyd's *Don't Call Me Madam* was the favourite at the time of the poll.

- Journalists dedicated an average of four hours and 57 minutes a week to their favourite books. When asked, most were reading Marquez's *One Hundred Years of Solitude*.

- Taxi drivers (four hours and 46 minutes) preferred biographies (33%), thrillers (24%) and true crime (12%).

- Lawyers (four hours and 33 minutes) were also great crime fans (41%), but they also lapped up gardening, poetry and self-help books.

- Teachers and chefs completed the list (four hours and 27 minutes). They also expressed a preference for Jane Austen and JRR Tolkien.

QUOTE UNQUOTE

There are three rules for writing the novel. Unfortunately, no one knows what they are.
W Somerset Maugham, novelist

LITERARY FESTIVALS

The intellectual heart of the August Edinburgh Festival, the **Edinburgh International Book Festival** (August, www.edinburgh-festivals.com) has been running for over 20 years. It started off as a biennial festival in 1983, becoming annual in 1997 and is now home to over 600 events during its fortnight run. Claiming to be 'the world's leading book festival', it certainly is one of the most intimate with talks and question-and-answer sessions held in a series of make-shift marquees in Charlotte Square.

COMMA SENSE

*'the nowing ones complane of my book the fust edition
had no stops I put in a nuf here and thay may peper
and solt it as they please'*

So complained Timothy Dexter when he reissued *A Pickle for the
Knowing Ones* (1802), a 24-page pamphlet, which had been
originally published without once using capital letters, full stops,
commas or any other form of punctuation. There was, however, one
small catch: rather than add it to the text, the author had simply
added another page at the end containing nothing but punctuation.
His contemporaries scoffed, but Dexter had the last laugh – the book
is now a rare collector's item.

WRITERS AND THEIR MUSES

If you think it's only the modern celebrity that chases the wrong skirt
(or trousers), think again; authors have been dipping their pens in forbidden inkwells for centuries...

A young **Lord Byron** was in love
with his cousin, Mary Cha-
worth, but unfortunately for him
she spurned his attentions.

WB Yeats was romantically
involved with Maud Gonne until
she married Major John
Macbride in 1903.

Franz Kafka had a stormy relationship with Felice Bauer to
whom he was engaged (and dis-
engaged) twice in five years.

Edgar Allan Poe lived with his
aunt and her 13-year-old daughter Virginia whom he subsequently married.

The fact that **Percy Bysshe Shelley**
was married did not stop him running off with Mary Woll-
stonecraft, who later authored
Frankenstein (1818). He was a
leading exponent of 'free love' and
although he eventually married
Mary in Paris, he hadn't actually
bothered to divorce his first wife.

Despite already being married,
Dante was involved in both his
personal life and in his writing
with a mysterious woman who
went by the name of Beatrice.

Oscar Wilde was imprisoned for
his affections towards young
blood Alfred 'Bosie' Douglas.

QUOTE UNQUOTE

*Resolve to edge in a little reading every day, if it is but a single
sentence. If you gain fifteen minutes a day, it will make itself felt at
the end of the year.*
Horace Mann, Father of US education

*Percentage of US viewers who said they were reading the Bible more as a
result of seeing the film* The Passion of The Christ *(2004)*

Improve your vocabulary, with the words in the Oxford English Dictionary that are immediately before and after writer names.

Bronco – a wild or untamed horse of the western US	Brontë, Anne Charlotte and Emily	**Brontosaurus** – dinosaur; from *bronte* thunder and *sauros* lizard
Camulodunum – the Roman name for Colchester	Albert Camus	**Camwood** – a red African wood
Fieldfare – a large thrush	Henry Fielding	**Field Marshal** – an officer of the highest rank in the British and other armies
Hellenistic – period of Greek history, language, and culture from the death of Alexander the Great in 323 BC to 31 BC	Joseph Heller	**Hellespont** – the ancient name for the Dardanelles (a narrow strait between Europe and Asiatic Turkey).
Lesser Sunda Islands – a chain of islands in the south-western part of the Malay Archipelago	Doris Lessing	**Les Six** – a group of six Parisian composers (Durey, Honegger, Milhaud, Tailleferre, Auric and Poulenc) formed after World War Two.
Kip (4) – small piece of wood from which coins are spun in the game of two-up	Rudyard Kipling	**Kipper** – a kippered fish, especially herring
Shaker – a person or a thing that shakes	Shakespeare	**Shakhty** – a coal-mining city in SW Russia
Shavuoth – the Jewish Pentecost	George Bernard Shaw	**Shaw** – the stalks and leaves of potatoes and turnips

POETIC PUZZLERS

Who first cried: 'Off with his head'?
Answer on page 153.

Number of letters CS Lewis wrote to editors during his lifetime 63

THE REWRITE WAS BETTER

The Old Man and the Tea
Santiago, an old Cuban fisherman, has the battle of his life
with a ferocious cup of Earl Grey.

LITERARY FEUDS

Many a strong friendship has died at the expense of ideas, and none
more so than two of France's most prodigious twentieth-century writers
and philosophers. Camus and Sartre met during the German occupation
of France in 1943, and quickly became friends. But as the Cold War
intensified, East–West relations drew them apart. Sartre believed in
violence as a means for change; Camus absolutely did not. They parted
as quickly as they met, following a brusque and public quarrel in 1952,
after which they never spoke again.

QUOTE UNQUOTE

Why don't you write books people can read?
Nora Joyce, to her husband James

WRITERS ON READING

All good books are alike in that they are truer than if they had really
happened and after you are finished reading one you will feel that all
that happened to you and afterwards it all belongs to you; the good
and the bad, the ecstasy, the remorse, and sorrow, the people and the
places and how the weather was.

Ernest Hemingway, 'Old Newsman Writes', *Esquire*

Less than a decade after Caxton was chipping his elaborate wood blocks of Chaucer's *Canterbury Tales* in 1483, Henry VIII was born. Henry's divorce from the Catholic Catherine of Aragon, four months after his marriage to Protestant Anne Boleyn put his succession in disarray, and caught his subjects between the censoring impulses of his royal daughters. Under the repressive instincts of the Catholic Queen Mary, Protestants had their works censored; under his youngest illegitimate daughter, Queen Elizabeth I, presses were instead offered to Protestant authors. So set the stage for printing controls.

In 1579 John Stubbs had his right hand cut off for illegally printing an attack on Elizabeth's marriage plans, while in 1633, the puritan William Prynne, had his ears cropped for publishing *Historio-Matrix*. Not surprisingly, when Prynne published his next volume, enticingly called *News from Ipswich*, he did so anonymously. Unfortunately his cover was blown and Charles I had the remaining ear stumps shorn off and the letters 'SL', for seditious libeller, branded on both cheeks.

Oliver Cromwell's revolution saw an end to Charles and a proliferation of the printed word, only to be again brought under royal control by the restored King Charles II, who executed at least one publisher, the unlucky John Twynn, hung drawn and quartered for an ill-timed volume on overthrowing the King.

Royal suppression did not last long. Emerging political parties saw the benefits of a political press through which they could disseminate their views. Restoration politicians were not, however, adverse to a little press control themselves. A year before the first English novel, Samuel Richardson's *Clarissa* appeared in 1740, parliament prevented books being imported to curtail the spread of any Irish political literature. Less repressive, but equally effective press controls came about with the Stamp Acts of the eighteenth century. These taxes on knowledge raised the costs of printing beyond all but the wealthiest publishers, stamping out working-class presses almost overnight.

Authors were also coming under a different type of scrutiny, spurred on by the moralistic concerns of the Victorian age. When Marguerite Radclyffe Hall's lesbian classic, *The Well of Loneliness* was published in 1928, the *Sunday Express* wrote that they 'would rather give a healthy boy a phial of prussic acid than this novel of unutterable putrefaction and contagion'. After the rush on sales the book was hastily banned.

But threats to censor do not always originate with the state. In 1989, it was Muslim radicals who threatened to kill Salman Rushdie after branding *The Satanic Verses* a 'libel against Islam'. Rushdie survived, but his Japanese translator was not so lucky. The novel was eventually published by an anonymous consortium.

TOP TEN LIBERIS PROHIBITORUM

The Adventures of Huckleberry Finn, **Mark Twain** (1884)
Banned on racial grounds and by Concord Public Library as 'trash suitable only for the slums'. When Twain was asked to defend the charges, he replied: 'I am greatly troubled by what you say. I wrote *Tom Sawyer* and *Huck Finn* for adults exclusively, and it always distressed me when I find that boys and girls have been allowed access to them. The mind that becomes soiled in youth can never again be washed clean.' Needless to say it needed a little more defending to avoid the ban.

Tropic of Cancer, **Henry Miller** (1934)
Banned until 1963 for sexual content and the preferred use of a four-letter word beginning with 'c', the book was first released in France on condition that the cover contain an explicit warning to book buyers. The publishers printed the advisories... on removable dust jackets.

Madame Bovary, **Gustave Flaubert** (1857)
Banned on sexual grounds. Prosecutor Ernest Pinard put it succinctly: 'No gauze for him, no veils – he gives us nature in all her nudity and crudity.'

Ulysses, **James Joyce** (1922)
TS Eliot described it as 'a book to which we are all indebted, and from which none of us can escape', but this didn't stop it being banned on sexual grounds in the USA and the UK.

The Kama Sutra
Banned for its sexual content, this Hindu holy book has caused no end of trouble for censors.

Lady Chatterley's Lover, **DH Lawrence** (1928)
Rumour has it that Lawrence purposefully used sexually explicit language in an effort to raise the ire of the UK censors. It worked. The book was subject to obscenity trials up to the 1960s.

Pistis Sophia
Banned for heresy, it was a capital offence in Europe and Asia to own a copy for more than 1,000 years.

The Satanic Verses, **Salman Rushdie** (1988)
Outlawed in Pakistan, Saudi Arabia, Egypt, Somalia, Sudan, Malaysia, Qatar, Indonesia, South Africa and India for its perceived criticism of Islam.

Frankenstein: a Modern Prometheus, **Mary Shelley** (1818)
Banned under South Africa's apartheid regime in 1955, for being 'indecent, objectionable, or obscene'. Anna Sewell's *Black Beauty* – a story about a horse – was also banned.

Lolita, **Vladimir Nabokov** (1955)
Nabokov broke one hell of a taboo when he published his now infamous 12th novel. It received a mixed response – Graham Greene considered it one of the best books of the year, while the *Daily Express* dismissed it as 'the filthiest book I've ever read'.

Speed reading isn't just about reading fast (that's 'skimming' apparently). You can actually attend courses that train you to read (and understand) not word-by-word but line-by-line and eventually paragraph-by-paragraph at breakneck speeds. Impatient readers should work their way through the following techniques:

The Hand
Place your right hand sideways on the page and, slowly and evenly, move it straight down the page, following smoothly with your eyes. Gradually increase the speed of your hand to increase the speed of your read.

The Card
Use a card above the line of print to block the words after you've read them. Be sure to push the card down faster than you think you can go and try to read the passage before the words are covered up.

The Sweep
Use your fingers to draw your eyes across the page by sweeping your hand from left to right in a fast, smooth motion under the line that you are reading.

The Hop
Similar to the sweep, except that with the hop you actually lift your fingers and make two even bounces on the line. This method also ensures a steady pace and rhythm.

The Zig-Zag
You know you've arrived when you master the zig-zag. It's the quickest form of scanning and allows you to cut across the text diagonally, picking up words in the whole paragraph rather than each word on a line.

The Skip
The ultimate in speed reading, this unauthorised technique involves jumping from the first to the last page with an optional stop on the middle page for a little more in the way of suspense.

LITERARY FESTIVITIES

At more than 50 years old, **The Cheltenham Festival of Literature** (October, www.cheltenhamfestivals.co.uk) is the longest-running festival of literature in the world. It's also one of the most comprehensive, with novelists, poets, dramatists, academics, biographers and even cartoonists taking the stage every year to present their works and answer questions from the audience. Launched in 1949 by local writer John Moore, today's event attracts a host of high-profile literary figures as well as political, showbiz and media personalities, and includes a popular children's festival, Book It!

WHAT THE DICKENS?

If you thought the death of Krook in *Bleak House* was the result of an over-active imagination, you may be mistaken. There were around 30 cases of 'spontaneous human combustion' on record when Charles Dickens was researching the death for *Bleak House* and (just to prove it isn't the naïvety of Victorian medicine), there have been another 200 non-fiction reports since.

One of the most famous cases occurred in St Petersburg, Florida in 1951. One 67-year-old Mary Hardy Reeser 'spontaneously combusted' while sitting in her easy chair and was found the next day in a blackened circle four feet in diameter. All that remained was a few blackened seat springs, a section of her backbone, a shrunken skull the size of a baseball, and one foot encased in a black slipper just beyond the four-foot circle. The police report declared that Mrs Reeser went up in smoke when her highly flammable rayon-acetate nightgown caught fire, perhaps because of a dropped cigarette, but as the rest of the apartment somehow managed to come through unsinged, nobody is entirely sure.

TOP TEN ODD BOOKS

Stéphane Mallarmé wrote 'everything in the world exists to end up in a book'; it seems he wasn't wrong...

The Unconscious Significance of Hair (George Berg, 1951)
How to Boil Water in a Paper Bag (Anon, 1891)
Teach Yourself Alcoholism (Meier Glatt, 1975)
How to Become a Schizophrenic (John Modrow, 1992)
Nuclear War: What's in it for you? (Ground Zero War Foundation, 1982)
A Pictorial Book of Tongue Coating (Anon, 1981)
Fish Who Answer the Telephone (YP Frolov, 1937)
The Thermodynamics of Pizza (Harold J Morowitz, 1991)
Who's Who in Barbed Wire (Anon, 1970)
Hand Grenade Throwing as a College Sport (Lewis Omer, 1918)

WRITERS ON READING

Read not to contradict and confute; nor to believe and take for granted; nor to find talk and discourse; but to weigh and consider. Some books are to be tasted, others to be swallowed, and some few to be chewed and digested: that is, some books are to be read only in parts, others to be read, but not curiously, and some few to be read wholly, and with diligence and attention.

Francis Bacon, *Essays, Civil and Moral*

68 *Year, in the nineteenth century, when Louisa May Alcott was asked by her publisher to write a 'book for girls'. The result was* Little Women.

THE REWRITE WAS BETTER

A Wail of Two Kitties
Two kittens warble their way through solitary confinement
during the French Revolution.

LITERARY LINGOS

Lapine (*Watership Down* – Richard Adams, 1972)
If Richard Adams is to be believed, beneath the fields and amid the
warrens of the idyllic English countryside much is being said. Lapine
– spoken by Hazel, Fiver, Bluebell and friends – is an intricately
conceived, yet beautifully simple naming language with not only its
own vocabulary but also a fully realised grammatical framework.

LAW STORY

Ernest Hemingway was once sued by a 70-year-old Cuban fisherman
named Miguel Ramirez who claimed that Hemingway's Pulitzer
Prize-winning novel, *The Old Man and the Sea* (1952), was an
unauthorised biography. The wily sea captain's not-altogether-
convincing case centred around his assertion that he had spent four
days chasing and catching a magnificent marlin in his youth, only to
have it eaten by sharks as he towed it back to shore. The suit was
thrown out after just a few minutes of thrashing around.

POETIC PUZZLERS

Who am I?
C
RAD
Answer on page 153.

THE ANGRY HOSHIBUDOU

Many an expression is lost in translation from English, but you'd expect the title of a novel to be converted with a fair bit of time and attention. Not so for John Steinbeck's *The Grapes of Wrath*, whose title (taken from the song 'The Battle Hymn of the Republic'), was translated into Japanese as 'the angry raisins'. John Steinbeck's widow was the first to pick up on the schoolboy error on a trip to Japan in 1989 to celebrate the 50th anniversary of the publication of the book. An especially appreciative fan dropped the clanger: 'We like your husband's work very much, particularly *The Angry Raisins*.' Apparently he would have been crushed.

QUOTE UNQUOTE

*Always read something that will make you look good
if you die in the middle of it.*
PJ O'Rourke, US humorist

A TWIST OF LEMON

Alcohol has been the inspiration for many a writer...

A Drink With Something In It (1935) –
Ogden Nash (on the benefits of a Martini)

Hangover Square (1941) – Patrick Hamilton

The Ordeal of Gilbert Pinford (1957) – Evelyn Waugh
(a tale based on a bout of hallucinations caused by alcohol and
sleeping tablets)

The Power and the Glory (1974) – Graham Greene
(his 'whiskey priest' chooses alcohol over God)

Under the Volcano (1947) – Malcolm Lowry
(considered by Stephen Spender to be one of the best accounts of a
'drunk' in fiction: 'Lowry shows us how a drunk thinks and feels,
walks and lies down, and we experience not only the befuddledness
of drinking but also its moments of translucent clairvoyance.')

Anything by Jack Kerouac, Dylan Thomas, Philip Larkin and Lord
'gin-and-water is the source of all my inspiration' Byron.

70 *Years after an author dies that their work enters the public domain and is
considered copyright free*

WHAT'S IN A NAME?

A good title, they say, is the title of a successful book, but it's not always easy to get there. Here are some working titles that didn't make the cut. The question is: would the novels still have hit the big time if the titles hadn't been changed?

A Portrait of the Artist as a Young Man (James Joyce, 1916)
Working Title: 'Stephen Hero'

Catch-22 (Joseph Heller, 1961)
Working Title: 'Catch-18'

David Copperfield
(Charles Dickens, 1849)
Working Title: 'Mag's Diversions'

The Great Gatsby
(F Scott Fitzgerald, 1925)
Working Title: 'Incident at West Egg'. Fitzgerald also suggested 'The High-Bouncing Lover' and 'Under the Red White and Blue', which his editor fortunately chose to ignore.

Gone with the Wind
(Margaret Mitchell, 1936)
Working Title: 'Ba! Ba! Black Sheep'

Northanger Abbey
(Jane Austen, 1798)
Working Title: 'Susan'

Portnoy's Complaint
(Philip Roth, 1969)
Working Title: 'A Jewish Patient Begins His Analysis'

Lady Chatterley's Lover
(DH Lawrence, 1928)
Working Title: 'John Thomas and Lady Jane'. Lawrence once mused that, but for its racy title, the book would not have been banned. Surely his proposed euphemisms wouldn't have fared much better.

Pride and Prejudice
(Jane Austen, 1831)
Working Title: 'First Impressions'

Sons and Lovers
(DH Lawrence, 1913)
Working Title: 'Paul Morel'

Treasure Island
(Robert Louis Stevenson, 1883)
Working Title: 'The Sea-Cook'

War and Peace
(Leo Tolstoy, 1866)
Working Title: 'All's Well that Ends Well' – not 'War: What is it good for?' as Elaine misinforms the cast in an episode of *Seinfeld*.

The Wasteland (TS Eliot, 1922)
Working Title: 'He do the Police in Different Voices'. It's a quote from Charles Dickens' *Our Mutual Friend*.

QUOTE UNQUOTE

Reading a book is like re-writing it for yourself... You bring to a novel – anything you read – all your experience of the world. You bring your history and you read it in your own terms.
Angela Carter, novelist

The contents of a bookshop according to Italo Calvino in *If on a winter's night a traveller:*

- Books You Haven't Read
- Books You Needn't Read
- Books Made For Purposes Other Than Reading
- Books Read Even Before You Open Them Since They Belong To The Category Of Books Read Before Being Written
- Books That If You Had More Than One Life You Would Certainly Also Read But Unfortunately Your Days Are Numbered
- Books You Mean To Read But There Are Others You Must Read First
- Books Too Expensive Now And You'll Wait Till They're Remaindered
- Books ditto When They Come Out In Paperback
- Books You Can Borrow From Somebody
- Books That Everybody's Read So It's As If You Had Read Them Too
- Books You've Been Planning To Read For Ages
- Books You've Been Hunting For Years Without Success
- Books Dealing With Something You're Working On At The Moment
- Books You Want To Own So They'll Be Handy Just In Case
- Books You Could Put Aside Maybe To Read This Summer
- Books You Need To Go With Other Books On Your Shelves
- Books That Fill You With Sudden, Inexplicable Curiosity, Not Easily Justified
- Books Read Long Ago Which It's Now Time To Reread
- Books You've Always Pretended To Have Read And Now It's Time To Sit Down And Really Read Them
- New Books Whose Author Or Subject Appeals To You
- New Books By Authors Or On Subjects Not New (for you or in general)
- New Books By Authors Or On Subjects Completely Unknown (at least to you)

QUOTE UNQUOTE

My notion of a great novel is something like a five-hundred-page shaggy-dog story, with only the punch line omitted.
Edward Abbey, US author

SMOKIE AND THE BROWNIE

Gertrude Stein famously created *The Autobiography of Alice B Toklas* (1933), but the subject, her lifelong companion Alice B Toklas, has also had her own share of literary fame. *The Alice B Toklas Cook Book*, which she put together in 1954, eight years after Stein's death, went down in urban legend thanks to one particularly hallucinogenic recipe. Presented as the 'Haschich Fudge, which anyone could whip up on a rainy day', her marijuana-laced brownies were to become the delicacy of choice in many a student kitchen. Here's the recipe, if you want to see what all the fuss was about:

Take one teaspoon black peppercorns, one whole nutmeg, four average sticks of cinnamon, one teaspoon coriander. These should all be pulverised in a mortar. About a handful each of stoned dates, dried figs, shelled almonds and peanuts: chop these and mix them together. A bunch of *canibus* [*sic*] *sativa* can be pulverised. This along with the spices should be dusted over the mixed fruit and nuts, kneaded together. About a cup of sugar dissolved in a big pat of butter. Rolled into a cake and cut into balls about the size of a walnut, it should be eaten with care. Two pieces are quite sufficient.

QUOTE UNQUOTE

I thought I'd begin by reading a poem by Shakespeare, but then I thought, why should I? He never reads any of mine.
Spike Milligan, comedian

POOP FICTION

Warning: these books may cause flatulence...

'Walter the Farting Dog' is a flatulent pooch whose little problem saves the day in the series of books by William Kotzwinkle and Glenn Murray which begin: 'Gas. He can't help it. It's just the way he is.'

In *The Adventures of Captain Underpants* our Y-fronted hero fights for truth, justice and all that is cotton with the motto: 'Never underestimate the power of underwear'. The brainchild of Dav Pilkey, the stories see his superhero attempting such dangerous challenges as leaping tall buildings without getting a wedgie and doing battle with the evil Professor Poopypants.

Andy Griffiths' *The Day my Butt Went Psycho* follows a 12-year-old named Zack whose backside is prone to detaching itself and making trouble. He followed it up with *Zombie Butts from Uranus*, in which Zack is again on hand to fight the butt fight to rid the earth of the stinky space invaders.

POETIC PUZZLERS

In HG Wells' *The Invisible Man*, who was the invisible man?
Answer on page 153.

WHERE CAN YOU FIND A FILING CABINET IN THE WONDERFUL WIZARD OF OZ?

Legend has it that L Frank Baum's make-believe land took its name from a cabinet drawer labelled O–Z, which was situated in front of him while he was putting his tale to paper. He corroborated the story in a press release for the book in 1903: 'I have a little cabinet letter file on my desk that is just in front of me. I was thinking and wondering about a title for the story, and had settled on the "Wizard" as part of it. My gaze was caught by the gilt letters on the three drawers of the cabinet. The first was A–G; the next drawer was labeled H–N; and on the last were the letters O–Z. And "Oz" it at once became.'

WRITERS ON READING

I saw a girl sitting on a stone bench near; she was bent over a book, on the perusal of which she seemed intent: from where I stood I could see the title – it was 'Rasselas'; a name that struck me as strange, and consequently attractive. In turning a leaf she happened to look up, and I said to her directly,

'Is your book interesting?' I had already formed the intention of asking her to lend it to me some day.

'I like it,' she answered, after a pause of a second or two, during which she examined me.

'What is it about?' I continued. I hardly know where I found the hardihood thus to open a conversation with a stranger; the step was contrary to my nature and habits: but I think her occupation touched a chord of sympathy somewhere; for I too liked reading though of a frivolous and childish kind; I could not digest or comprehend the serious or substantial.

'You may look at it,' replied the girl, offering me the book.

I did so; a brief examination convinced me that the contents were less taking than the title: 'Rasselas' looked dull to my trifling taste; I saw nothing about fairies, nothing about genii; no bright variety seemed spread over the closely-printed pages. I returned it to her; she received it quietly, and without saying anything she was about to relapse into her former studious mood.

Charlotte Brontë, *Jane Eyre*

BURNING ISSUES

If you're not going to do it properly, don't do it all, or so thought Virgil whose quest for perfection nearly ended in the burning of his 12-book Latin classic *The Aeneid*. The epic, which tells the story of the Trojan prince Aeneas and his wanderings, which led to the foundation of Rome, was 11 years in the writing when the author fell ill returning from a trip to Greece. He had intended to spend another three years editing it into shape and, loathe to let it be published as it stood, demanded on his deathbed that the manuscript be destroyed. Fortunately, the Roman emperor Augustus – who had commissioned the piece – stepped in and arranged for the poem to be published.

Virgil isn't the only author to seek to destroy his written legacy. Franz Kafka also requested that all his work be destroyed just before his death from tuberculosis in 1924.

QUOTE UNQUOTE

The only demand I make of my reader is that he devote his whole life to reading my works.
James Joyce, novelist

LIBRARIES WITH A DIFFERENCE

In Kenya, the Camel Library Service brings books to about one million people in isolated villages around the city of Garissa. Since its launch in 1996, the fleet has grown from three to six camels.

The Chilean bookworm Horacio Ogaz travels the outskirts of Chañaral on a tricycle heavily laden with books with his door-to-door library service. However, he's not the only mobile book deliverer in Chile; the 'Book Adventurers' fill their suitcases and backpacks with books to bring the library to the people in Olivar Alto.

In Zimbabwe, remote communities are supplied with services such as book loans, radio, telephone, fax and the internet by 'donkey drawn electro-communication library carts'.

Floating libraries carry books to people in Alaska, Norway, Sweden and Thailand. Alaska's Kusko Book Express (KBE) reported distributing over 5,000 books to more than 1,150 students in 2003.

Although there are bookcases in the entrance halls, The Library in Las Vegas isn't a place to visit for books. The kind of learning that goes on here is a more revealing affair: it comes courtesy of librarians who strip rather than shush.

PC PRONOUNS

In an article published in January 1912 by *The Chicago Tribune*, educational reformer and suffragist Ella Flagg Young proposed the use of alternative gender pronouns to make the English language less biased against women. Editors everywhere would have been grateful if she had devised something elegant and useful; but as her suggestions were his'er, he'er, him'er and his'er's, the alternatives, sadly, were doomed never to catch on.

Young wasn't the first to tackle the issue of gender-neutral pronouns; around 80 new terms have been suggested since the 1850s, but none have made any visible headway in popular usage. In 1884, the composer Charles Converse's proposals (thon and thons) made their way into several unabridged dictionaries, but they were dropped soon after. 'Sie', 'hir', 'ey', 'zie' and 'hesheit' met similar fates.

QUOTE UNQUOTE

He who lends a book is an idiot.
He who returns the book is more of an idiot.
Arab Proverb

NOT IN THEIR LIFETIME

Success is sweet, but sometimes it can come that little bit too late...

The Collected Poems – Sylvia Plath (1981)
Plath's Pulitzer Prize-winning collected works were published 18 years after her death in 1963. poetry was published post-humously to instant success, transforming her from a 'forgotten poetess' to 'the greatest American poet of the nineteenth century' almost overnight.

The Leopard – Giuseppe Tomaso di Lampedusa (1958)
When the Sicilian nobleman Giuseppe Tomaso di Lampedusa died in 1957, he left the completed (and previously rejected) manuscript of *The Leopard* in his drawer. It was published shortly after and quickly became a success.

Poems – Dante Rossetti (1870)
When his wife died, Rossetti decided to bury his manuscript of poems with her. Seven years later he changed his mind, so he disinterred the poems and had them published to great acclaim.

Unpublished Poems – Emily Dickinson (1935)
Comparatively unnoticed during her lifetime, Dickinson's

Pensées – Blaise Pascal (1670)
In *Pensées*, Pascal tried to answer that all-important question – why are we here? – but didn't manage to get it out in his own lifetime.

Time, in years, that Charles Lamb's Little Masterpieces *(1899) was overdue at Salt Lake City Public Library before it was returned*

BOOKSHOP STORIES

Shakespeare & Co
Two bookshops, two movements, one spirit...

In 1921, Sylvia Beach founded Shakespeare & Co at 12, rue de l'Odeon, Paris, and through it introduced writers Ernest Hemingway and F Scott Fitzgerald to European readers. As well as providing a meeting place for the collection of writers who would become known as the Lost Generation, Beach sealed her shop's place in literary history by agreeing to publish James Joyce's *Ulysses*, then regarded by publishing houses as little more than pornographic filth. Needless to say the gamble paid off.

In 1941, with Paris under Nazi occupation, Shakespeare & Co was threatened with closure when Beach refused to sell a copy of *Finnegan's Wake* to a German officer. Rather than risk the destruction of her stock,

Beach mobilised her friends and in the two hours it took the officer to return, all trace of the bookshop had vanished.

Twenty-three years later, George Whitman, the owner of a bookshop at 37, rue de la Bûcherie, sought Beach's permission to resurrect her company's name and spirit. With permission granted, Whitman continued his commitment to writers by installing beds among the books, thereby providing the accommodation that can still be enjoyed today. In exchange for his hospitality, Whitman (now in his nineties and an enigmatic character who singes his hair shorter with the flame of a candle) only asks for an hour of work per day and a commitment to match his prolific reading habits.

THE BEST WRITER FOR THE JOB

The Able Coincidence – JN Chance (1969)
Alpine Plants of Distinction – A Bloom (1968)
Anatomy of the Brain – WW Looney (1932)
Criminal Life – Superintendent J Bent (1891)
Crocheting Novelty Pot-holders – L Macho (1982)
Common Truths from Queer Texts – Reverend J Gay (1908)
Electronics for Schools – RA Sparkes (1972)
Grace of God – A Lord (1859)
Inside Story – A Dick (1943)
The Principles of Insect Philosophy – VB Wigglesworth (1939)
Spices from the Lord's Garden – Reverend EID Pepper (1895)
A Treatise on Madness – W Battie MD (1758)
Violence Against Wives – Emerson and Russell Dobash (1979)
The World of My Books – IM Wise (1954)

THE REWRITE WAS BETTER

Vanity Chair
The ruthless Becky Sharp defies her impoverished
background to clamber up the class ladder and nab
herself an elegant chaise longue.

WRITERS ON READING

At evening when the lamp is lit,
Around the fire my parents sit;
They sit at home and talk and sing,
And do not play at anything.

Now with my little gun I crawl,
All in the dark, along the wall.
And follow round the forest track
Away behind the sofa back.

There in the night, where none can spy,
All in my hunter's camp I lie,
And play at books that I have read,
Till it is time to go to bed.

*   *   *   *

So, when my nurse comes in for me,
Home I return across the sea,
And go to bed with backward looks
At my dear Land of Story Books.
Robert Louis Stevenson, *The Land of Story Books*

LIPOGYMNASTICS

As if writing a novel wasn't difficult enough in itself, some authors have chosen to make the task that little bit more taxing by adding an extra hurdle. The practice of lipograms (derived from the Greek for 'omit') sees a writer deliberately exclude a letter of the alphabet by avoiding all words that include that letter. It's even harder than it sounds...

The Greek poet **Tryphiodorus** started the craze when he wrote *The Odyssey* by missing out a different letter of the alphabet from each of the 24 books.

Following in his footsteps, sixteenth century French clergyman **Peter de Riga** wrote a summary of the Bible in which a different letter of the alphabet was excluded from each of the 23 chapters.

As the title of **Jacques Arago's** *Voyage autour du monde sans la lettre A* ('Journey around the world without the letter A', 1853) suggests, this worldly tale was written without using the letter 'a'. However, the author did later confess that a single use of the word 'serait' (would be) had managed to creep in and spoil his near-perfect endeavour.

Cuddly bear-hugger **Gyles Brandreth** is a huge lipogram fan. He rewrote *Hamlet* without using the letter 'i', *Macbeth* without 'a' or 'e', *Twelfth Night* without 'i' or 'o' and *Othello* without 'o' (except in the titles it would seem).

Ross Eckler's hobby was rewriting well-known nursery rhymes excluding certain letters. His favourite was *Mary Had a Little Lamb* which he recreated in several versions including one without the 't' entitled *Mary Had a Pygmy Lamb*.

Ernest Vincent Wright's *Gadsby* (1939) is surely one of the most impressive. Wright wrote this novel of more than 50,000 words without once using the letter 'e'. It took six months to create and presumably a lot of determination – 'e' is the most commonly used letter in the English alphabet.

The French author **Georges Perec** hit the headlines in 1990 when he published another 'e'-less novel, this time *La disparition* (translated into English as 'a void' and not the literal 'the disappearance' for obvious reasons).

Mark Dunn offered the most recent example of the art in 2000. In *Ella Minnow Pea*, his characters communicate through a series of letters and notes, which progressively decrease in their use of certain letters.

German Romantic poet **Gottlob Burmann** so despised the letter 'r' that not only did he write 130 poems without once using it, he also insisted on excluding it from everyday conversation. Presumably if anyone asked his name, he would just reply, 'Gottlob "B"'.

MAKING ENDS MEET

Before fame, many a writer has been forced into the odd period of nine-to-five; here are some before-they-were-famous occupations, some of them little known...

Joseph Conrad was a merchant sailor for 20 years.

Salman Rushdie spent many a year working in advertising. He thought up the cream cakes strap line 'Naughty but nice'.

Sylvia Plath worked as a receptionist at a psychiatric clinic.

John Milton was appointed Secretary for the Foreign Tongues.

In 1970, **Hunter S Thompson** stood for election of Sheriff of Pitkin, Colorado, with a 'freak power' campaign. He lost by a handful of votes.

Thomas Hardy trained as an architect.

While broadcasting wartime propaganda for the BBC during World War Two, **Orwell** worked in an office numbered 101. He also served as a British Civil Servant in India for 20 years and as an officer of the Indian Imperial Police in Burma for five years.

Lewis Carroll was deacon and maths teacher at Oxford.

Edgar Allan Poe spent a number of years editing and writing for magazines and newspapers. Unfortunately, his inability to hold his liquor got him fired from each job.

Kingsley Amis supplemented his income as a university lecturer.

Charles Dickens first worked as a court stenographer and a shoe factory worker.

TS Eliot was rather boringly a clerk at Lloyds Bank.

JRR Tolkien was professor of English at Oxford University.

LITERARY PRIZES

The most prestigious award available to British novelists, the Booker Prize, has secured the fame and fortune of many a previous winner – not least the 2002 victor Yann Martel for the *Life of Pi*. Any novel written by a citizen of the United Kingdom, the Republic of Ireland, or the British Commonwealth is eligible to enter and win the £21,000 prize as long as it is published in the English language and first released in the United Kingdom. The 1981 award winner, Salman Rushdie's *Midnight's Children*, currently holds the title for the 'Booker of Bookers', it was named the outstanding Booker winner of the first 25 years of the competition in 1993.

POET'S CORNER

Part of the south transept of Westminster Abbey, Poet's Corner, contains the tombs and monuments of many of Britain's most distinguished authors, playwrights and poets...

Geoffrey Chaucer
Chaucer was the first to be buried in the Abbey but he wasn't buried here for his literary accomplishments: he was Clerk of Works to the palace of Westminster.

Edmund Spenser
Spenser was the second: his burial started the tradition of burying poets, writers and playwrights near each other in the Abbey.

Rudyard Kipling • Richard Brinsley Sheridan
Samuel Johnson • Thomas Hardy • John Dryden
Alfred Lord Tennyson • Robert Browning
John Masefield • Samuel Johnson • Charles Dickens

Although they are not actually buried here, there are also memorials to Lord Byron, William Shakespeare, John Milton, William Wordsworth, Thomas Gray, John Keats, Percy Bysshe Shelley, Robert Burns, William Blake, TS Eliot and Gerard Manley Hopkins; and writers such as Samuel Butler, Jane Austen, Oliver Goldsmith, Sir Walter Scott, Charlotte, Emily and Anne Brontë, Henry James and Sir John Betjeman.

GONE WITH THE WIND

Three novels have been credited with sales of over 30 million, all of them by American female authors. The top best-sellers are *Gone with the Wind* (1936) by Margaret Mitchell, *To Kill a Mockingbird* (1960) by Harper Lee and *Valley of the Dolls* (1966) by Jacqueline Susann.

EVEN HARRY POTTER WON'T DO

When Scottish teenagers were asked about their reading habits in 2000 by the Organisation for Economic Co-operation and Development (OECD), the results were astonishing. A third of teens said they 'never' or 'hardly ever' read for pleasure, a fifth considered reading 'a waste of their time', and 40% said they only read if they had to. The figures emerged from an international study of 15-year-olds from across 28 countries, which fortunately also revealed that Scottish pupils were in the top six in the international reading literacy rankings. The findings also showed that teen Scots were much more likely to read magazines or newspapers than they were to read books – with 80% claiming to have read newspapers at least several times in the last month.

ONE-HIT WONDERS

As in the world of pop music, having one best-seller doesn't guarantee you can (or want to) write a second success...

Wuthering Heights
(Emily Brontë, 1847)

Gone with the Wind
(Margaret Mitchell, 1936)

To Kill a Mockingbird
(Harper Lee, 1960)
Three quintessential one-hit wonders.

The Catcher in the Rye
(JD Salinger, 1951)
Although it is rumoured that Salinger is still writing, he went into hiding after the success of his debut novel and only collections of short stories have been seen since.

Tropic of Cancer
(Henry Miller, 1934)
The wild, self-confessional and notorious narrative of an impoverished expat's existence in Paris, this one-hit wonder also suffered at the hand of the literary sensors.

Invisible Man
(Ralph Ellison, 1952)
For 40 years Ellison tried to write another work, filling filing cabinets and computer disks with manuscripts and notes, but died without managing to make the manuscript coherent enough to be understood. His work was eventually edited down and published after his death as *Juneteenth* (1999).

Catch-22 (Joseph Heller, 1961)
Catch-22 wasn't Heller's only book, but he never wrote anything that managed to come out of its shadow. But then, as he once replied to an interviewer who pointed this out: 'Who has?'

Ring of Bright Water
(Gavin Maxwell, 1960)
Maxwell's tales of his life in a cottage in the remote Highlands sold three million copies, but although he went on to publish further works, he never managed to shake off the 'otter man' tag – he even had a type of otter named after him, the *Lutrogale perspicillata maxwelli*.

Under the Volcano
(Malcolm Lowry, 1947)
Under the Volcano was the only novel published by Lowry in his lifetime – it took him 20 years to write it and he killed himself shortly after.

QUOTE UNQUOTE

Borrowers of books – those mutilators of collections, spoilers of the symmetry of shelves, and creators of odd volumes.
Charles Lamb, British essayist and poet

HELP WITH HOBBIES

Creative activities worth considering...

The Art and Craft of Pounding Flowers: No Paint, No Ink, Just a Hammer! (Laura Martin, 2001)

The Great Pantyhose Crafts Book (Edward Baldwin, 1982)

Woodcarving with a Chainsaw (Lyn Mangan, 1998)

Lightweight Sandwich Construction (JM Davies, 2001)

More Tea Bag Folding (Tiny van der Plas, 2001)

Original Tricks with Cigars (Micky Hades, 1927)

Pranks with the Mouth (Anon, 1879)

Explosive Spiders and How to Make Them (John Scoffern, 1881)

Levitation for Terrestrials (Robert Kingsley Morison, 1977)

Collect Fungi on Stamps (DJ Aggersberg, 1997)

Let's Make some Undies (Marion Hall, 1954)

How to Cook Husbands (Elizabeth Stong Worthington, 1899)

One Hundred and Forty-one Ways of Spelling Birmingham (William Hamper, 1880)

Play With Your Own Marbles (JJ Wright, SW Partridge, c.1865)

WHEN MIDDLE BECAME MODERN

Sometime during the fifteenth or sixteenth centuries, Middle English became modern English with the dramatic change in vowel pronunciations that l. since become known as the 'Great Vowel Shift'. The Middle English long 'i' (formerly pronounced like the modern 'e') shifted to the current 'i' as in high, the Middle English 'sheep' (formerly pronounced 'shape') changed to the modern 'sheep' and the Middle English 'hous' (pronounced 'hoose') to the modern 'house' in a general movement forward of 'long' vowel sounds in the mouth.

The change happened so fast that only 50 years after Geoffrey Chaucer wrote *The Canterbury Tales*, his readers were pronouncing his words in completely different ways.

WHERE DO YOU READ?

A survey of 1,000 British people for Bedtime Reading Week 2002 found the most popular place to read was in bed (65% of readers). 25% liked to relax with a book in the bath, 10% preferred to take a book to the toilet (mainly men), almost half liked to read on holiday and a third read on the journey to work. More than a third said they wished they had more time to read.

Harry Potter uses *The Standard Book of Spells* by Miranda Goshawk in the JK Rowling children's books.

The Duke's Daughter was written by central character Jo March in Louisa May Alcott's *Little Women*. The money she made from it went to pay the butcher's bill.

On the Polyphonic Motets of Lassus, *On the Surface Anatomy of the Human Ear* and *Upon the Uses of Dogs in the Work of the Detective* are all the imaginary brainchildren of Arthur Conan Doyle's Sherlock Holmes.

Well, that about wraps it up for God, Where God Went Wrong, Some More of God's Greatest Mistakes and *Who is this God Person Anyway?* by Oolon Colluphid are all referred to in Douglas Adams' *A Hitchhiker's Guide to the Galaxy*. Adams explains Oolon's grudge against God in an episode where his pregnant mother is given a fright by a pair of Jehovah's witnesses.

Protagonist Humbert Humbert writes *Lolita, or the Confession of a White Widowed Male* in Vladimir Nabokov's *Lolita*.

Bilbo Baggins works on *The Red Book of Westmarch* (aka *The Red Book of Periannath*) in JRR Tolkien's *The Hobbit* and *The Lord of the Rings*.

Speculations on the Source of the Hampstead Ponds, With some Observations on the Theory of Tittlebats is the literary construction of Samuel Pickwick in Charles Dickens' novel *The Pickwick Papers*.

Milo Temesvar's *On the Use of Mirrors in the Game of Chess* is referred to in Umberto Eco's *The Name of the Rose* and De Amicis' *Chronicles of the Zodiac* in Eco's *Foucault's Pendulum* despite the fact that neither the books nor their authors exist.

Is Man a Myth?, *Men, Monks and Gamekeepers: a Study in Popular Legend* and *The Life and Letters of Silenus* are all to be found in Mr Tumnus' cave in *The Lion, the Witch and the Wardrobe*.

The works of fictional Victorian poets Randolph Henry Ash and Christabel LaMotte guide the story of the real-life novel *Possession: A Romance*, by AS Byatt.

Advanced Ass-licking for Graduate Students, *The Proper Method of Farting in Company*, *The Law's Codpiece* and *How to Keep it up until You're Ninety* (among others) appear in Rabelais' *Gargantua and Pantagruel*.

Fictional alter-ego Kilgore Trout creates the science fiction works of *The Gospel from Outer Space*, *Venus on the Half-Shell*, and *Now it can be Told* in Kurt Vonnegut's series of books.

Number of days, in Hemingway's The Old Man and the Sea *(1952), that Santiago had gone without catching any fish*

THE REWRITE WAS BETTER

The Camomile Prawn
Mary Wesley records the story of one crustacean's
adventures in London during the Blitz.

LITERARY LINGOS

Nadsat (*A Clockwork Orange* – Anthony Burgess, 1962)
A cacophony of Russian and German, of gypsy and cockney slang,
and of schoolboy baby talk, Nadsat (the Russian suffix for -teen) is
the unintelligible language of Alex de Large and his marauding
cohorts. It's a harsh dialect that reflects an even harsher detachment
between anti-hero and the 'respectable' society that spawned him.
Can you figure it out?

> *We gave this devotchka a tolchock on the litso*
> *and the krovvy came out of her mouth*
> (We gave this girl a blow on the face
> and blood came out of her mouth).

LITERARY FEUDS

'Take it on the chin, dear fellow, and move on.'
So spoke VS Naipaul to his friend and protégé Paul Theroux after
Theroux found one of his first editions, inscribed to Naipaul, listed for
sale in a rare-book catalogue at £1,500. The two have argued ever since.

WRITERS ON READING

There are people who read too much: bibliobibuli. I know some who are constantly drunk on books, as other men are drunk on whiskey or religion. They wander through this most diverting and stimulating of worlds in a haze, seeing nothing and hearing nothing.

HL Mencken, *Minority Report: HL Mencken's Notebooks*

THE SUBTEXT

Subtitles that got lost somewhere along the way...

Black Beauty: The Autobiography of a Horse (Anna Sewell, 1877)
Brideshead Revisited: The Sacred and Profane Memories of Captain Charles Ryder (Evelyn Waugh, 1945)
The Hunting of the Snark: An Agony in Eight Fits
(Lewis Carroll, 1876)
Fanny Hill: Memoirs of a Woman of Pleasure (John Cleland, 1748)
Frankenstein, or the Modern Prometheus
(Mary Wollstonecraft Shelley, 1818)
The Hobbit: There and Back Again (JRR Tolkien, 1937)
Gulliver's Travels, or Travels into Several Remote Nations of the World (Jonathan Swift, 1726)
Man and Superman: A Comedy and a Philosophy
(George Bernard Shaw, 1903)
Pamela, or Virtue Rewarded (Samuel Richardson, 1740)
Slaughterhouse-Five, or Children's Crusade, a Duty Dance with Death (Kurt Vonnegut, 1969)
Roots: the Saga of an American Family (Alex Haley, 1976)
Tess of the D'Urbervilles: A Pure Woman Faithfully Presented
(Thomas Hardy, 1891)
Twelfth Night, or What You Will (William Shakespeare)
Vanity Fair: A Novel without a Hero (William M Thackeray, 1847)

THE ICE MAN

Since most early literate civilisations were located in warm climes, the first mention of an iceberg in literature didn't occur until the ninth century. It was an Irish traveller, the monk St Brendan who first recorded the phenomenon of a 'floating mountain of glass' (although he did not know what it was) in *Navigatio Sancti Brendani* ('Voyage of St Brendan'). But Brendan isn't just known for recording the first sight of an ice mountain, faithful followers also believe that the saint discovered the continent of America. He reported a new island far to the west in his writings and, added to the maps of that era, may have given the first indication of its existence to Columbus.

Hundreds of meaningless words litter our lives, but what about those common experiences, feelings and situations, which no word can adequately describe? In *The Meaning of Liff and The Deeper Meaning of Liff*, Douglas Adams and John Lloyd solve the problem by ambushing the names of our towns and reapplying them where they are needed most. Here are their thoughts on all things literary...

Ahenny *(adj.)* – the way people stand when examining other people's bookshelves.

Ainderby Quernhow *(n.)* – One who continually bemoans the 'loss' of the word 'gay' to the English language, even thought they had never used the word in any context at all until they started complaining they couldn't use it anymore.

Ballycumper *(n.)* – one of the six half-read books lying somewhere in your bed.

Bathel *(vb.)* – to pretend to have read the book under discussion when in fact you've only seen the TV series.

Beppy *(n.)* – the triumphal slamming shut of a book after reading the final page.

Dalmilling *(ptcpl.vb.)* – continually making small talk to someone who is trying to read a book.

Fritham *(n.)* – a paragraph that gets you stuck in a book. The more you read it, the less it means to you.

Great Wakering *(ptcpl.vb.)* – the panic which sets in when you badly need to go to the lavatory and cannot make up your mind about what book or magazine to take with you.

Great Tosson *(n.)* – a fat book containing four words and six cartoons which costs £12.95.

Liff (n.) – a book, the contents of which are totally belied by its cover. For instance, any book the dust jacket of which bears the words, 'This book will change your life'.

Pulverbatch *(n.)* – the first paragraph on the blurb of a dust-jacket in which famous authors claim to have had a series of menial jobs in their youth.

Ripon *(vb.)* – to include all the best jokes from the book in a review to make it look as if the critic thought of them.

QUOTE UNQUOTE

What really knocks me out is a book that, when you're all done reading it, you wish the author that wrote it was a terrific friend of yours and you could call him up on the phone whenever you felt like it. That doesn't happen much, though.
JD Salinger, US novelist

QUOTE UNQUOTE

*I know every book of mine by its smell, and I have but to put my
nose between the pages to be reminded of all sorts of things.*
George Robert Gissing, English novelist

BROUGHT TO BOOK

In 2004, the Canadian portal of Amazon.com accidentally published
the real identity of the writers of 'anonymous customer reviews'.
Several well-known authors who had promoted their own works and
trashed those of their rivals were unmasked. Among them were John
Rechy (*City of Night*, 1963) who wrote as 'a reader from Chicago' of
the merits of his work *The Life and Adventures of Lyle Clemens* (to
which he awarded five stars) and Dave 'a reader from St Louis'
Eggers, author of *A Heartbreaking Work of Staggering Genius*, who
wrote a gushing review of a work by his friend Heidi Julavits. It's all
a far cry from the experiences of Rick Moody, author of *The Ice
Storm,* who once wrote of a particularly harsh review posted by his
mother on Amazon.com: 'She gave me three out of five stars... and
then she told me that it was a *positive* review.'

POETIC PUZZLERS

Which of his novels did Charles Dickens say he liked the best?
Answer on page 153.

PICK UP A PENGUIN

Paperback books have been
around since the seventeenth
century, but they really began to
take off with the first 10 Penguins
released by Allen Lane in London
in 1935. With the motto 'Good
books cheap', they cost sixpence
a volume – the cheapest a quality
book had ever been sold for.

The Penguin symbol was
designed by Edward Young in
1935 to mark the spines of the
first launches of Penguin fiction.

In the early years, colour coding
of Penguin covers was used to
denote the category of book:
orange for fiction; green for
crime; light blue for non-fiction;
dark blue for biography; cerise
for travel; red for theatre; and
yellow for miscellany.

The Penguin Pelican imprint was
launched in 1937 with grand
aplomb. The books were sold in
a Penguincubator, a new
paperback dispenser, on Charing
Cross Road.

In 1956, Lane created Puffins, a
series of paperback books
expressly written for children.

Edgar Allan Poe became the first author of a detective story in the English language when he wrote *The Murders in the Rue Morgue* in 1841. However, European literary historians trace the genre back to the earlier *Zadig* (1747) by French author Voltaire.

The first English detective mystery was *The Moonstone* (1868) by **Wilkie Collins**. It charts the disappearance of a priceless Indian diamond and a puzzling murder, which uses all the classic elements of the genre including red herrings, alibis and sufficiently-heavy clues for the reader to solve the crime ahead of its hero, Sergeant Cuff of Scotland Yard.

Sherlock Holmes was first introduced to the world in *A Study in Scarlet* in *Beeton's Christmas Annual* in 1887. But, even though **Arthur Conan Doyle** was one of the leading exponents of the detective story, he later got tired of his hero and bumped him off in *The Final Problem* in 1893, after a struggle with archenemy Professor Moriarty. Fans didn't take the death as well as he had hoped and he eventually brought the character back in *The Adventure of Empty House* (1903).

Dubbed the Queen of Crime by her millions of fans, **Agatha Christie**'s first detective novel *The Mysterious Affair at Styles* (1920) featured the moustached Belgium charmer, Hercule Poirot. Miss Marple appeared for the first time in 1930 in *Murder at the Vicarage* by which time Christie was well on her way to becoming one of the most successful mystery writers of the twentieth century. Christie formed part of the 'Big Four', a group of successful female detective storywriters that also included Dorothy L Sayers, Ngaio Marsh and Margery Allingham.

After World War Two, the 'tougher' US style of crime fiction ended the 'Golden Age' of the British detective story as writers turned to tales of crime and spying. **Colin Dexter**'s Inspector Morse, who first appeared in *Last Bus to Woodstock* (1975), formed part of the genre's move from sleuth 'as hobby' to that of sleuth 'as occupation', which came as a reaction to the increasing lack of plausibility in earlier tales. From such tales also sprang up the sub-genre of 'police procedural', in which a complete crime unit is depicted concurrently investigating a series of separate crimes.

One of the most prolific mystery writers, **Carolyn Keene** of Nancy Drew fame, wasn't even a real person. The series, first published by Grosset and Dunlap, was written by dozens of ghost-writers hired by Stratemeyer Syndicate who submitted the novels under the pen name 'Carolyn Keene'.

PEN PALS

Just to prove the green-eyed monster can be kept at bay, here are some of literature's most famous writing buddies...

Kingsley Amis and Phillip Larkin

Wordsworth and Coleridge

Coleridge remarked that William and Dorothy Wordsworth and himself were 'three persons and one soul'.

TS Eliot and Ezra Pound

Jack Kerouac and Neal Cassady

James Boswell and Samuel Johnson

Franz Kafka and Max Brod

Jack London and Joseph Conrad

Ted Hughes and Seamus Heaney

Henry Miller and Michael Fraenkel

Both made a pact that their correspondence could not end until, together, they had completed one thousand pages of letter writing. Miller may have wanted to see an end to the bet – his final letter was more than 100 pages long.

Ernest Hemingway and F Scott Fitzgerald

Percy Bysshe Shelley and John Keats

WRITERS ON READING

It has long been my belief that everyone's library contains an Odd Shelf. On this shelf rests a small, mysterious corpus of volumes, whose subject matter is completely unrelated to the rest of the library, yet which, upon closer inspection, reveals a good deal about its owner. George Orwell's Odd Shelf held a collection of bound sets of ladies' magazines from the 1860s, which he liked to read in his bathtub. Philip Larkin had an especially capricious Odd Shelf crammed with pornography, with an emphasis on spanking. Vice Admiral James Stockdale, having heard that Frederick the Great had never embarked on a campaign without a copy of *The Encheiridion*, brought to Vietnam the complete works of Epictetus, whose Stoic philosophy was to sustain him through eight years as a prisoner of war.

Anne Fadiman, *Ex Libris, Confessions of a Common Reader*

QUOTE UNQUOTE

I was working on the proof of one of my poems all the morning, and took out a comma. In the afternoon I put it back again.
Oscar Wilde, British playwright

LITERARY LINGOS

Newspeak (*1984* – George Orwell, 1949)
The official language of Oceania, concocted to further the ideological aims of IngSoc (English Socialism) and make all other expression impossible, was widely expected to replace Oldspeak by the middle of the twenty-first century. Riddled with logical contradictions while being grammatically regular, Newspeak was designed to eliminate the possibility of heretical thoughts. The ninth and tenth editions of Orwell's fictitious *Newspeak Dictionary* included such entries as Airstrip One (the new name for an England dominated by the USA), blackwhite (the ability to accept whatever 'truth' the party puts out, no matter how absurd it may be), duckspeak (to speak without thinking) and, of course, Room 101 (the final punishment for 'thoughtcriminals' in the Ministry of Love).

POETIC PUZZLERS

In Camus' *L'Etranger*, who was the stranger?
Answer on page 153.

READ WITH MOTHER

The nation's favourite children's poems according to a 2001 BBC poll...

1. *The Owl and the Pussy Cat* – Edward Lear
2. *Matilda* – Hilaire Belloc
3. *Don't* – Michael Rosen
4. *Jabberwocky* – Lewis Carroll
5. *On the Ning Nang Nong* – Spike Milligan
6. *Talking Turkeys!!* – Benjamin Zephaniah
7. *Macavity the Mystery Cat* – TS Eliot
8. *The King's Breakfast* – AA Milne
9. *Please Mrs Butler* – Allan Ahlberg
10. *Down with Children! Do Them In!* – Roald Dahl

ANAGRAM ANARCHY

Just before the first print run of *Under Milk Wood*, Dylan Thomas altered the name of his Welsh fishing village from Llareggub to Llareggyb. Why the last-minute change? Thomas suddenly realised that, when reversed, the original name spelled 'Buggerall'.

Year, in the nineteenth century, that Herman Melville, creator of 91
Moby Dick, died

WHEN TO JUDGE A BOOK BY ITS COVER

Over the years, books have been bound in some of the most fitting of materials:

Asbestos – *Fahrenheit 451* (Ray Bradbury, 1953)

Black lace panties – *Grand Opening: A Year in the Life of a Total Wife* (Alice Whitman Leeds, 1980)

Cigar box – *The Soverane Herbe: A History of Tobacco* (WA Penn, 1901)

Cricket blazer – *Baxter's Second Innings* (Henry Drummond, 1892)

Fish skin – *The Compleat Angler* (Izaak Walton, 1653)

Handkerchief – *The Love Sonnets of a Hoodlum* (Wallace Irwin, 1901)

Human skin – *Poetical Works* (John Milton, 1645)

Bound in the skin of a murderer, Milton's wasn't the only work to befit such a cover. During the French Revolution, a copy of the new constitution was bound with the tanned leather skin of a guillotined aristocrat.

Japanese Silk – *Quicksilver (*Neal Stephenson, 2003)

Skunk skin – *Mein Kampf* (Adolf Hitler, 1925)

Plywood – *Modern Plywood* (Thomas D Perry, 1942)

Sheets – *The Rise and Fall of Carol Banks* (Elliott W Springs, 1931)

Soldier's uniform – *All Quiet on the Western Front* (Erich Maria Remarque, 1929)

WRITERS ON WRITING

Like any other organism, language changes. It lives in the real world and gets knocked about from time to time. It adapts in order to survive. Look up almost any word in the Oxford English Dictionary and you can follow the journey that it has taken over the centuries, changing its precise meaning as it twists and turns with the passing of time. Often its present meaning bears little relationship to its original one. It is silly to imagine that this evolution can be halted. It is even sillier to try...

There are so many threats to the survival of good, plain English that it is not easy to be optimistic. Email has a great deal to answer for. Punctuation is no longer required and verbs are abandoned with the speed of a striptease artiste late for her next performance. Text messaging is worse – much worse. Yet I have seen it suggested that students be allowed to use "texting" abbreviations in examinations. Ultimately, no doubt, we shall communicate with a series of grunts – and the evolutionary wheel will have turned full circle.

John Humphrys in the introduction to James Cochrane's
Between You And I: A Little Book of Bad English

PSEUDONYMS FOR LIFE

Authors who first created their names and then penned their works...

Voltaire – Francois-Marie Arouet
Stendhal – Marie-Henri Beyle
Anthony Burgess – John Wilson
Lewis Carroll – Charles Lutwidge Dodgson
Dodgson created his pen name by transposing and Latinizing his first two names.
Molière – Jean Baptiste Poquelin
George Orwell – Eric Arthur Blair
Dr Seuss – Theodore Seuss Geisel
Mark Twain – Samuel Langhorn Clemens
John le Carré – David Cornwell
Katherine Mansfield – Katherine Beauchamp
Daniel Defoe – Daniel Foe
Jack London – John Griffith
Enid Blyton – Mrs Daryl Walters

MALAPROPISMS

From *mal à propos* (French for inappropriate), the comical (and unintended) misuse of words was first brought to the stage by the self-educated Mrs Malaprop in Sheridan's 1775 Restoration comedy, *The Rivals*. Here are some of her best:

'...promise to forget this fellow – to illiterate him, I say, quite from your memory.' (obliterate)
'O, he will dissolve my mystery!' (resolve)
'He is the very pine-apple of politeness!' (pinnacle)
'I have since laid Sir Anthony's preposition before her.' (proposition)
'Why, murder's the matter! slaughter's the matter! killing's the matter! – but he can tell you the perpendiculars.' (particulars)

MUFFIN MATTERS

There's a champion on hand for all those book readers who have spent their literary lives chastised for creasing the book spine, folding over the corners to keep their page or spilling coffee and dropping crumbs on their newest read. Charles Lamb is one of many who believed that a book kept in pristine condition couldn't match one we've left our fingerprints on. 'A book reads the better,' he wrote, 'which is our own, and has been so long known to us, that we know the topography of its blots, and dog's ears, and we can trace the dirt in it to having read it at tea with buttered muffins.'

The heir to the British throne was tentatively accused in 2003 of penning a goonish series of Amazon.com reader reviews under the pseudonym of Henry Raddick. The reviews, which puzzled and amused internet users over the 18 months it took for the organisation to get wind of the spoofs, first appeared under the name of Andrew Lloyd Webber (including personal endorsements for books on combating halitosis and premature ejaculation), but when Webber threatened to sue, the secretive scribbler was forced into a name change. Is Prince Charles really Henry Raddick? The jury's still out...

Raddick's Reviews:
The Art of Flamenco by David George, et al
I bought this book for my wife. Flamenco is the dust of the bull-ring, the flounce of the gypsy's skirt and the crazy clatter of castanets. Flamenco swaggers. Flamenco pleads. Flamenco is the beating heart of Andalusia. Flamenco is NOT a tanked-up Englishwoman embarrassing her husband in a hotel bar in Seville.

The 5 Reasons Why We Overeat: How to Develop a Long-Term Weight-Control Plan That's Right for You by Cynthia G. Last
Last's superb guide enables the reader to identify which 'eating profile' they fall into, and thereby select the weight-loss strategy appropriate to them. With my wife, who really let herself go quite some time ago, 'Remorseless Grazer' covers most of the angles – and to know this is to be prepared. I found it easy to read and well thought out, and we certainly need it after Marjorie ballooned massively over our two week Second Honeymoon.

You Can Teach Your Dog to Eliminate on Command by M L Smith, Syd Stibbard (Illustrator)
Smith and Stybbard have written a gem in this book. It's certainly helped me to take control of my dog's idiosyncratic toilet habits. My pug Grendel now dances to my tune, be it on walks, in the garden or merely impressing friends and family. A word of caution – take care when choosing your 'command words' and 'smart phrases' to avoid words your dog is likely to hear on the television. It took four episodes of Ali [sic] McBeal before I realised that my 'full evacuation' command was in the theme song.

Surviving Divorce: A Handbook for Men by Gay Search
A well-written and challenging book which I bought for my Uncle Sandy as he attempts to cope with the aftershock of divorce. Unfortunately, he thought the author's name was the coping strategy being suggested and he refused to read it.

QUOTE UNQUOTE

*The most essential gift for a good writer
is a built-in shock-proof shit-detector.*
Ernest Hemingway, US novelist

CREATIVE COCK-UPS

When *The Lord of the Rings* was published in 1950, JRR Tolkien, then professor of ancient languages at Oxford, may have been slightly surprised to learn that it would eventually sell more than 100 million copies. But he was certainly surprised by the cover illustration used for the first American paperback edition. 'I think the cover ugly,' he wrote to his publisher at Ballantine, 'but I recognise that a main object of a paperback cover is to attract purchases, and I suppose that you are better judges of what is attractive in the USA than I am. I therefore will not enter into a debate about taste, but I must ask this about the vignette: What has it got to do with the story? Where is this place? Why a lion and emus? And what is the thing in the foreground with pink bulbs? I do not understand how anybody who had read the tale (I hope you are one) could think such a picture would please the author.'

When Tolkien later confronted his publisher, he found his concerns to be justified – neither the illustrator nor the publisher had 'had time' to read the work.

BRITAIN'S TOP PUBLIC INTELLECTUALS

When British monthly, *Prospect* magazine, asked: 'Who are Britain's top 100 public intellectuals?' in 2004, the following literary types made the list:

Martin Amis (novelist and critic) • Melvyn Bragg (broadcaster and writer) • AS Byatt (critic and writer) • John Carey (literature professor and critic) • Matthew D'Ancona (journalist and writer) • Terry Eagleton (literary theorist) • Michael Frayn (playwright and novelist) AC Grayling (philosopher, writer and journalist) • Germaine Greer (writer and feminist) • David Hare (playwright)
Seamus Heaney (poet) • Frank Kermode (literary critic and writer) Ian McEwan (novelist) • VS Naipaul (novelist and essayist)
Melanie Phillips (author and columnist) • Philip Pullman (children's author) • Salman Rushdie (writer)
Roger Scruton (philosopher and writer) • Gitta Sereny (biographer) George Steiner (writer and academic) • Tom Stoppard (playwright) Jeanette Winterson (novelist) • James Wood (literary critic)

PLAY-IT-SAFE NOM DE PLUME

Why risk your hard earned reputation just because you want to try something new? Here are some high-working authors who thought they'd play it on the safe side...

Amnesia Glasscock
John Steinbeck published *The Collected Poems* (1976) under this forgettable name.

Mary Westmacott
Agatha Christie tried her hand at gothic romances under this nom de plume, but the books – *Unfinished Portrait*, *The Rose and the Yew Tree* and *A Daughter's Daughter* – didn't attain anywhere near the fame of the writer's mysteries.

Jane Somers
Doris Lessing's *The Diaries* (1984) were published under this name.

Richard Bachman
When Stephen King released *Thinner* (1984) under the pseudonym Richard Bachman, one literary review described the book as 'what Stephen King would write like, if Stephen King could really write'. There were plenty of red faces when the 'real' author was revealed.

Victoria Lucas
Sylvia Plath released her only novel, *The Bell Jar*, under this assumed name.

Robert Markham
The penname Kingsley Amis used for his James Bond novel *Colonel Sun* (1968).

Alcofri bas Nasier
François Rabelais created his penname out of an anagram of his own name to release the classic *Gargantua and Pantagruel*.

LIBRARY FINES

Library fines vary from city to city and from borough to borough, but here's roughly what you can expect to pay...

Ten pence per day per item for the first week the item is overdue
Forty pence per week after the first week
Maximum fine: **£10 per item**

Exemptions from fines apply to senior citizens (60 years and over), children and young adults (18 years and younger), members on state benefits (Jobseekers Allowance or income support) and users of the Mobile Library.

If you don't have the time to drop off the books, you can always renew your books over the phone. Books can be renewed up to three times without bringing them back to the library, unless they have been reserved by another borrower.

THE REWRITE WAS BETTER

The Cat is the Hat

LITERARY BANDWAGONS

The Bloomsbury Group

During the years between 1904 and World War Two, a number of Cambridge graduates would meet with their closest friends for drinks and conversation in Bloomsbury. This informal gathering subsequently became known as an immensely creative, productive and influential meeting of minds. With Virginia Woolf, EM Forster, Lytton Strachey and John Meynard Keynes among its members, the Bloomsbury group was committed to a rejection of Victorian values on all fronts – moral, artistic and sexual. Resented by some as a snobbish clique, The Bloomsbury group has since become just as famous for the romantic entanglements of several of its members as it has for their individual creative achievements.

THE POWER AND THE GLORY

When *Book Club News* ran a competition offering a prize for the best parody of Graham Greene's work in 1949, the entries came in thick and fast. After selecting and publishing a winner, the magazine was surprised to receive a letter from the author himself: 'While I was overjoyed that Mr John Smith had won the contest,' Greene wrote, 'I felt that John Doakes and William Jones were also deserving of prizes.' Greene had sent in all three entries – they were rejected passages from earlier works.

Victor Hugo was a madman who thought he was Victor Hugo. *Jean Cocteau*

The high-water mark, so to speak, of Socialist literature is WH Auden, a sort of gutless Kipling. *George Orwell*

I was reading Proust for the first time. Very poor stuff. I think he was mentally defective. *Evelyn Waugh*

Kingsley Amis once said that sex is a great cure for a hangover, which, indeed must be the case, because if you thought Kingsley Amis was going to make love to you, you'd certainly avoid getting drunk in the first place. *Joseph O'Connor*

Mr Wordsworth never ruined anyone's morals, unless, perhaps, he has driven some susceptible persons to a crime in the very fury of boredom. *Erza Pound*

A demagogic Welsh masturbator who failed to pay his bills *Robert Graves on Dylan Thomas*

There are two ways of disliking poetry. One way is to dislike it; the other is to read Pope. *Oscar Wilde*

If you imagine a Scotch commercial traveller in a Scotch commercial hotel leaning on the bar and calling the barmaid Dearie, then you will know the keynote of Burns' verse. *AE Housman*

Joseph Heller's *God Knows* even looks exactly like a real book, with pages and print and dust jacket and everything. This disguise is extremely clever, considering the contents; the longest lounge act never performed in the history of the Catskills. *Paul Gray*

HG Wells throws information at the reader as if emptying his mind like a perpetual chamber pot from a window. *Henry James*

Mr C had talent, but he couldn't spel. No man had a right to be a lit'rary man onless he knows how to spel. It is a pity that Chawcer, who had geneyus, was so unedicated. He's the wus speller I know of. *Artumus Ward*

It is the most insipid ridiculous play that ever I saw in my life. *Samuel Pepys, in his Diary (29 September 1662) after viewing A Midsummer's Night Dream*

With the single exception of Homer, there is no eminent writer, not even Sir Walter Scott, whom I can despise so entirely as Shakespear. *George Bernard Shaw (who always insisted on spelling Shakespeare without the final 'e').*

THE REWRITE WAS BETTER

King Solomon's Waistlines
An elephant hunter's chronicle of his safari into the interior of
South Africa and its effects on his ever-expanding belly.

LITERARY BANDWAGONS

The Lost Generation

Named by Gertrude Stein and led (in public perception at least) by
Ernest Hemingway, the young writers who sailed from the USA for
Paris shortly after World War One – beset with post-war
disillusionment and the first clawings of twentieth-century ennui – left
in search of creative fulfilment and the bohemian lifestyle. And, for
the most part, they found it. Drinking, writing and copulating their
way around Paris, Hemingway, John Dos Passos, F Scott Fitzgerald
and Henry Miller (to name the brightest stars among many),
challenged literary convention with mixed success. Not that 'success'
was ever really the issue, as Miller declares in *Tropic of Cancer*: 'I am
not interested in perfecting my thoughts nor my action... It is the
triumph of the individual over art.'

POETIC PUZZLERS

In the DH Lawrence novel, who was Lady Chatterley's lover?
Answer on page 153.

A TALE OF TWO INMATES

Marco Polo (1254–1324), author of one of the Western world's most famous travelogues, may not even have written it down on paper if he hadn't been captured by the Genoese and imprisoned for a year. Three years after Marco returned to Venice from his historic 24-year adventure in the Far and Middle East, he was captured during fighting with the rival city of Genova, where he found himself holed up with a writer of romances named Rustichello di Pisa.

It was only when prompted by Rustichello that Marco Polo dictated the story of his travels, which, published as *The Description of the World or The Travels of Marco Polo*, became one of the most popular books in medieval Europe.

QUOTE UNQUOTE

I took a speed-reading course and read War and Peace *in 20 minutes. It involves Russia.*
Woody Allen, filmmaker

WRITERS ON WRITING

'MY dear sir,' said the editor to the man, who had called to see about his poem, 'I regret to say that owing to an unfortunate altercation in this office the greater part of your manuscript is illegible; a bottle of ink was upset upon it, blotting out all but the first line – that is to say – *The autumn leaves were falling, falling.*

'Unluckily, not having read the poem, I was unable to supply the incidents that followed; otherwise we could have given them in our own words. If the news is not stale, and has not already appeared in the other papers, perhaps you will kindly relate what occurred, while I make notes of it.

'*The autumn leaves were falling, falling.* Go on.'

'What!' said the poet, 'do you expect me to reproduce the entire poem from memory?'

'Only the substance of it – just the leading facts. We will add whatever is necessary in the way of amplification and embellishment. It will detain you but a moment.

'*The autumn leaves were falling, falling...* Now, then.'

There was a sound of a slow getting up and going away. The chronicler of passing events sat through it, motionless, with suspended pen; and when the movement was complete Poesy was represented in that place by nothing but a warm spot on the wooden chair.

Ambrose Bierce,
'The Poet and the Editor', *Fantastic Fables*

Life expectancy, in years, of books currently being produced; the sulphuric acid in the wood pulp paper rots rapidly

POETIC CRIB

Blank Verse	a verse with no rhyme but plenty of meter. The form tends to favour ten-syllable iambic pentameters as used by Shakespeare in his dramas and by Milton in *Paradise Lost*.
Clerihew	a pair of couplets that rhyme AABB and usually describe a person.
Concrete poetry	free-form verse, relying heavily upon its visual impact on the printed page.
Limerick	a five-line jingle rhymed AABBA.
Haiku	a Japanese lyric of 17 syllables split into three lines of five, seven and five syllables.
Heroic couplets	a two-line couplet in iambic pentameter often used in epic and narrative poetry.
Epic	a continuous narrative poem, celebrating a hero or an event.
Ode	a poem, originally intended to be sung, addressed to someone or something.
Sonnet	a poem of 14 lines. A Shakespearean sonnet splits the 14 lines into three groups of four and follows them with a couplet (rhyming ABAB CDCD EFEF GG); a Miltonic sonnet splits the 14 lines into two groups of eight and six (rhyming ABBAABBA CDECDE).

CARRY AND CASH

If you've ever wondered whether an author gets paid for the reading of books borrowed from public libraries, then the answer is yes. The Public Lending Right Act came into being in 1979 after years of writers complaining that they didn't receive a penny in profit no matter how many times their books were borrowed from a library. The act entitled the author to a payment – currently just over four pence per book up to a maximum of £6,000 – per issue. To make it easier to enforce, royalties are based on a carefully monitored sample of libraries throughout Britain.

QUOTE UNQUOTE

The man who doesn't read good books has no advantage over the man who can't read them.
Mark Twain, US novelist

LITERARY LINGOS

Tlön, Uqbar and Tertius Orbis
(*Labyrinths* – Jorge Luis Borges, 1964)

A single mention in an out-of-print edition of the *Encyclopedia Britannica* is all Borges initially had to fuel his interest in the planet Tlön and its mysterious languages – some that are without verbs, others without nouns. As years pass, however, and chance experience repeatedly throws up interesting titbits about this planet so profoundly different from Earth, he still comes no closer to establishing whether Tlön, and it's languages like Tertius Orbis, ever actually existed or whether they are just the elaborate construct of a renegade intellectual clique.

THE WORST WITCH

The magical tale of an orphaned boy who discovers his wizard heritage at an unusual boarding school for magicians has won the hearts of millions, and the suspicions of a few. Pottermania, it seems, has a dark side.

At its strongest in the USA, a growing movement is targeting the seven-book series for the propagation of the word of the devil. They contend that the books are merely Satan's cover in his ultimate plan to plant immorality and corruption in the minds of the nation's children. Christian societies are becoming passionately divided on the issue, schools are banning them on the grounds that they are sacreligious and entire families are refusing to buy them because the occult skills they allegedly contain (witchcraft, sorcery, casting spells, spiritualism, interpreting omens and 'calling up the dead') are considered 'an abomination to the Lord'.

It appears that the UK's most beloved young hero isn't quite as humble and courageous as was once thought.

CREATIVE COCK-UPS

Experimental writer Gertrude Stein has had her share of mockery for her loose and rambling writing style, and no more so than from her editor, AJ Fifield, who sent her the following rejection: 'I am only one, only one, only one. Only one being, one at the same time. Not two, not three, only one. Only one life to live, only 60 minutes in one hour. Only one pair of eyes. Only one brain. Only one being. Being only one, having only one pair of eyes, having only one time, having only one life, I cannot read your MS three or four times. Not even one time. Only one look, only one look is enough. Hardly one copy would sell here. Hardly one. Hardly one.'

SPELLING IT OUT

Literacy facts from the National Literacy Trust...

• According to the *CIA World Fact Book*, the UK adult population is 99.6% literate. It estimates that there are 802 million illiterate adults in the world, two thirds are whom are women.

• When literacy is tested in practical situations, more adults perform poorly in the UK than in many other industrialised societies. Twenty-three per cent of UK adults have problems at the lowest level, compared to Sweden where it is only 7%. Ireland is 1% worse-off than the UK, the USA 1% better.

• Of those who have problems, 93.2% have difficulty with spelling and 39.8% with writing. When tested 68% of the population misspelt accommodation, including 53% of graduates.

• In the 2002 Literacy in the Age of Information report, Britain ranked 16th out of 22 in tests of quantative literacy (understanding figures and statistics), 15th out of 22 in tests of document literacy (understanding how to fill out forms) and 13th out of 22 in tests of prose literacy (understanding newspapers and stories). The countries who ranked lower than the UK were Hungary, Poland, Slovenia, Portugal and Chile.

• Surveys of literacy attainment have been carried out in the UK since 1948. Their main finding is that literacy standards have changed very little in that time.

WRITERS ON READING

She buried herself in the 'Corbeille', a woman's paper, and the 'Sylphe des Salons'. She devoured, without skipping a word, all the accounts of first nights, race meetings and fashionable 'at homes'. She got excited about the 'debut' of a new operatic star or the opening of a new shop. She was up in all the latest fashions, knew where the best tailors were, the days for the Bois and the days for the Opera. She gloated over the descriptions of furniture in the novels of Eugene Sue; she read Balzac and George Sand, seeking some imaginary balm for the longings of her heart. She would even bring her book with her to table and go on turning the pages while Charles ate and talked. And as she read, the memory of the Vicomte continually came back to her. She compared and likened him to the characters in the books. But the circle of which he was the centre, gradually enlarged around him, and the aureole which encompassed him withdrew farther and farther from him, to shed its light on other dreams.

Gustave Flaubert, *Madame Bovary*

*Books have to be read (worse luck it takes so long a time).
It is the only way of discovering what they contain. A few
savage tribes eat them, but reading is the only method of
assimilation revealed to the West.*
EM Forster, novelist

NEW WRITING DEFINITIONS

An anonymous posting on the internet and a work of sheer brilliance...

Autobiography	Car maintenance manual.
Copyright	'This is okay to copy, right?'
Ghost writing	The number of books, articles, stories that you have written in your head but are yet to commit to paper.
Headline	Wrinkly bits on forehead caused by writing deadlines.
Lead	What you use to walk your dog while formulating new ideas.
Love scene	Said when you finally write a good paragraph: 'I love that scene'.
Playwright	Play computer Solitaire 90% : write 10%
Procrastination	An oxymoron because it begins immediately after you land an assignment.
Publication	When a critic pans your book in their newspaper review.
Referfence	When an interviewee falls through so you replace them with your neighbour.
Science faction	Science fiction writing for the unimaginative.
Womanuscript	Feminine of manuscript.

LITERARY FEUDS

Influential philosopher Jean-Jacques Rousseau launched a career by advocating the 'innate goodness of humans', but it seems he didn't always quite believe what he preached. When David Hume, Scotland's prized philosopher, invited Rousseau to England in 1766, the French intellectual became increasingly convinced that Hume, his friend and benefactor, and the British government's spies and guards were set on killing him. After a year in his paranoid company, Hume understandably retracted his earlier assertion that 'there is no man in Europe of whom I have entertained a higher idea'.

THE GREAT PRETENDERS

In 2004, as a counterpoint to the BBC survey of the nation's 100 favourite novels, John Walsh in *The Independent* asked his famous pals to do the exact opposite – to nominate the books they wished that they had never read. Here are some of the best, and most surprising:

The Lord of the Rings by JRR Tolkien
Anything about Gandalf, and those little things with hair between their toes. I hate that sort of portentous, phoney, medieval-magical way of writing.
Sir John Mortimer: Author and creator of Rumpole

Ulysses by James Joyce
I always failed to get very far with this. It's one of those books you think you ought to read because everyone says it's such a classic, but it's completely incomprehensible. I found it impenetrable and I got fed up with the style. It's been decades since I tried to read it, and I don't think I'll bother trying again. *Neil Hamilton: Disgraced former Conservative minister*

The Harry Potter books by JK Rowling
I think they are absolute shit, just terrible, worse than Enid Blyton. I have discouraged my children from reading them. They are not particularly badly written – I don't mind bad writing – it's the smugness and the complicity with the reader that I dislike. It's like they're written by a focus group. JK Rowling is the sub-literary analogue of Tony Blair. *Jonathan Meades: Author and broadcaster*

Possession by AS Byatt
It's a kind of schmaltzy Mills & Boon romance dressed up with cod Victorian poetry to make it seem more profound, but there's no emotional depth in it at all. It's incredibly shallow and trivial. *Joan Smith, Author*

The Last Place on Earth: The complete story of the dramatic race for the Pole by Roland Huntford
If you know the facts, you wince as you turn the pages. Huntford's diatribe against Scott of the Antarctic is a benchmark in ill-informed denigration hiding under the cloak of historical research. *Sir Ranulph Fiennes: Explorer*

A Brief History of Time by Stephen Hawking
You think you understand it, but then you get to the end, and realise you don't. *Tony Banks: Labour MP for West Ham*

QUOTE UNQUOTE

A book is a fragile creature. It suffers the wear of time, it fears rodents, the elements, clumsy hands.
Umberto Eco, Italian novelist

PUB FICTION

Chaucer's pilgrims begin their journey from **The Tabard** in Southwark in his *Canterbury Tales*. His wasn't a literary creation, the popular coaching inn existed until 1873.

Shakespeare's Falstaff often drank at **The Boar's Head** in Eastcheap in the City of London. The Boar's Head actually existed, although it was knocked down in 1830 to make way for the new London Bridge road.

Mary Ann Sailors and grandson Sinbad keep **The Sailor's Arms** in Dylan Thomas' *Under Milk Wood*. It's always open – the clock has been stuck at 11.30pm for the last 50 years.

In Oliver Goldsmith's *She Stoops to Conquer*, Tony Lumpkin can be found drinking in **The Three Jolly Pigeons**.

Miss Abbey Potterton keeps **The Six Jolly Fellowship Porters** in Limehouse in Dicken's *Our Mutual Friend*.

The family of Jim Hawkins keep an inn called **The Admiral Benbow** in Robert Louis Stevenson's *Treasure Island*.

George Orwell first described **The Moon under Water** in an essay in the *Evening Standard* (1946). The name has since been adopted for a chain of pubs operated by JD Wetherspoon.

THE FIVE FATHERS

Daniel Defoe – Father of Modern Prose Fiction
Henry Fielding – Co-Father of the English Novel
Ben Jonson – Father of Poets
Edgar Allan Poe – Father of the Detective Story
Samuel Richardson – Co-Father of the English Novel

BOOKS IN HIGH PLACES

Just to prove running the country isn't a full-time job, four-time Prime Minister William Ewart Gladstone also managed to devise in his free time a storage system now in use in the Bodleian Library in Oxford. On *Books and the Housing of Them* (1898), a brief 29-page study of the looming problems of book shelving at the major libraries of the time even went right down to studies of the spacing of shelves, what size lumber to use and how to organise your collection. As if that isn't enough, Gladstone also offers recommendations on the proper of style of binding to match the book and which books should never share the same shelf; such as Conservative and Labour manifestos, perhaps.

TOP TEN EUPHEMISMS FOR ROMANCE FANS

10. Her heaving breasts
9. His punishing kiss
8. Her liquid centre
7. His rigid member
6. Her sensitive bud
5. His stirring loin
4. Her nubbin of flesh
3. His throbbing manhood
2. Her bucking hips
1. His growl of release

TONGUE TWISTERS

The longest word in the English language, according
to the Oxford English Dictionary, is
pneumonoultramicroscopicsilicovolcanoconiosis.

The only other word with the same amount of letters is
pneumonoultramicroscopicsilicovolcanoconioses,
the plural form.

WRITERS ON WRITING

I have come legally to man's estate. I have attained the dignity of
twenty-one. But this is a sort of dignity that may be thrust upon one.
Let me think what I have achieved.

I have tamed that savage stenographic mystery. I make a
respectable income by it. I am in high repute for my accomplishment
in all pertaining to the art, and am joined with eleven others in reporting the debates in Parliament for a Morning Newspaper. Night after
night, I record predictions that never come to pass, professions that
are never fulfilled, explanations that are only meant to mystify. I wal-
low in words. Britannia, that unfortunate female, is always before me,
like a trussed fowl: skewered through and through with office-pens,
and bound hand and foot with red tape. I am sufficiently behind the
scenes to know the worth of political life. I am quite an Infidel about
it, and shall never be converted...

I have taken with fear and trembling to authorship. I wrote a little
something, in secret, and sent it to a magazine, and it was published
in the magazine. Since then, I have taken heart to write a good many
trifling pieces. Now, I am regularly paid for them. Altogether, I am
well off, when I tell my income on the fingers of my left hand, I pass
the third finger and take in the fourth to the middle joint.

Charles Dickens, *David Copperfield*

QUOTE UNQUOTE

*A sequel is an admission that you've been
reduced to imitating yourself.*
Don Marquis, US journalist and short story writer

THE REWRITE WAS BETTER

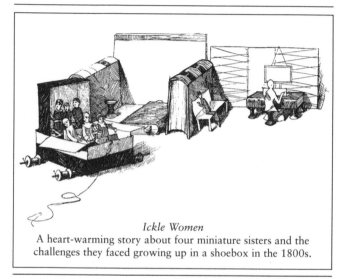

Ickle Women
A heart-warming story about four miniature sisters and the
challenges they faced growing up in a shoebox in the 1800s.

POETIC PUZZLERS

In the Shakespeare play, who was the merchant of Venice?
Answer on page 153.

LITERARY FEUDS

It seems even Vladimir Nabokov, the quintessential European
intellectual aristocrat, couldn't escape the pettiness of minor
quibbling. His friendship with former mentor, the influential literary
critic and young editor of *The New Republic*, Edmund Wilson, fell
foul of a dose of creative criticism. Nabokov asked for his friend's
'honest' opinion on the pre-release copy of *Lolita* (and we all know
what that really means), to which Wilson replied: 'I like it less than
anything else of yours I have read' and called the characters and
situations 'repulsive' and 'unreal'. Nabokov's nymphet made history,
but so did their feud – they argued to their deathbeds.

Poet: What would you like to ask?
Schoolgirl: Well. What's it about?
Poet: What's the poem about?
Schoolgirl: Yeah. What's it about?
Poet: Hmm... I suppose you could say it's about it's about it's about let's see. The speaker, or narrator, who may or may not be me, note... well all right I suppose it is me but it doesn't necessarily follow it is anyway... The narrator. Is. Someone who's woken up on a Sunday morning having obviously you know enjoyed himself wahay on the previous Saturday night if-ya-know-what-I-mean, I expect you do! so, right, so what I mean is is he's dealing with a hangover that's in the second stanza those are hangover cures or they're not, nothing's is, at least I find. Sleep maybe. But you know what a hangover is, don't you, right yes, you do, of course ha ha, maybe you've got one right now! maybe not, no of course, no. You haven't, you're you're 13. And I'm anyway fourth stanza. I haven't either of course, fourth stanza he's feeling sort of wired, sort of sensitive you could say, and he's suffering, he feels like he's got one skin less than you know, the average, er, skin allocation, and he cares what people say, that's an aspect certainly – of it. So he wanders around the house, sort of not engaging with this or that, feeling kind of existential – er... feeling kind of like an existing you know thing, thinking about himself like in the universe, alone in it, with as I say, that skin thing, from earlier. And the breathing, obviously. That regular, sort of, measure like a, I don't know, like a... listen. Can't hear it... And he what, I'm just checking it now he, he can't sleep, on top of all that he's lying there or sitting there and he can't sleep, he looks out of the window see in the middle of the eight stanza, eight stanza... Stanza. Italian for room. He's in a room, just as he's in a oh GOD...

             Sorry, little sip of water, that's good, Volvic, so he looks out, away, off, out at his own town, which is you know, just like your own town, but it's my own town as opposed to, as opposed to... and he's there, there with his water, and he takes a you know a pill to sleep which ends his his his consciousness his awareness as it indeed it ends the poem at that very exact point because beyond it there's only the see for yourself the well the the the whiteness.
Schoolgirl: Why didn't you just write that then?

**Glyn Maxwell in *Mortification: Writers' Stories
of their Public Shame* edited by Robin Robertson**

GAOL BOOKS

Great literature to have emerged from behind bars...

In the Belly of the Beast: Letters from Prison
Jack Henry Abbott (1981)
A powerful book that became all the more notorious after Abbott committed another murder shortly after his early release.

The Pilgrim's Progress
John Bunyan (1684)
Imprisoned over long periods for preaching without a licence, Bunyan had plenty of time to think this one up.

Letters and Papers from Prison
Dietrich Bonhoeffer (1951)
Imprisoned for his part in a plot to assassinate Hitler, Bonhoeffer spent his time creating this crucial work of modern theology.

The Prince
Machiavelli (1513)
Machiavelli conceived this royal tome after he had been wrongly imprisoned for forming a rebellion against Florence's ruling Medici family.

Our Lady of the Flowers
Jean Genet (1949)
Notorious French thief and male prostitute, Genet spent most of his youth in prison putting this novel to paper.

On the Yard
Malcolm Braly (1967)
A frightening insight into a US penitentiary by a former inmate of San Quentin.

Don Quixote
Miguel de Cervantes (1615)
Banged up for his debts, Cervantes may have conceived of this classic as a route to financial freedom.

De Profundis
Oscar Wilde (1905)
Wilde is often mistakenly thought to have penned *The Ballad of Reading Gaol* when he was trapped inside it for two years. But what he actually created was this miserable tale of a life gone wrong.

MORE MONKEY, WITH LESS ART

A million monkeys, a million typewriters, and sooner or later a simian will have bashed out the scripts for any one of Shakespeare's plays, according to the Infinite-Monkey Theorem. First popularised by astrophysicist Sir Arthur Eddington, and then featured by Russell Maloney in his short story *Inflexible Logic*, the idea was also featured in *The Hitchhiker's Guide to the Galaxy*, when an infinite number of monkeys ambush the crew for their opinion on the monkey's script for *Hamlet*. The online Monkey Shakespeare Java Simulator (http://user.tninet.se/~ecf599g/aardasnails/java/Monkey/webpages) sets the current record at 16 letters.

Amount, in pounds, that Jane Austen received from publisher Thomas Egerton for Pride and Prejudice *(1813)*

The modern term 'dictionary' came to English from the Latin '*dictionarium*' through the French 'dictionnaire', which properly means 'book of sayings'. It was first used c.1225 by English scholar John Garland as the title for a manuscript of Latin words to be learned by memory. The synonym 'lexicon' comes from Greek and means 'book of words'. Lexicography refers to the act or process of making a dictionary.

The earliest lexicographers were monks. Before the printing press was invented, they worked in church libraries making notes in the margins of their hand-written books to clarify the Latin terminology for their less-educated brethren. These notes were known as 'glosses' from where we get the word 'glossary' – meaning a list of words with definitions.

In the earliest dictionaries, the words were not arranged in alphabetical order but grouped according to subject. The first alphabetical edition was published in 1604 by English schoolmaster Robert Cawdrey and entitled *A Table Alphabeticall conteyning and teaching the true writing and understanding of hard usual English Wordes... with the interpretation thereof by plaine English words, gathered for the benefit & helpe of Ladies, Gentlewomen, or any other unskilfull persons.*

The English dictionary as we know it today grew out of Samuel Johnson's *A Dictionary of the English Language* (1755). So confident was Johnson of his literary powers that he offered to write the dictionary in three years even though it had earlier taken 40 French scholars 40 years to create a French equivalent. He went over his target, but not by that much, finishing the work in just eight years.

Noah Webster is credited with being the 'father' of American dictionaries. He objected to the 'personal' and 'hasty' style of Samuel Johnson's work and his *A Compendious Dictionary of the English Language* (1806) set the standard for the regimented system for lexicography that continues to this day.

Webster is also the man responsible for respelling the 'our' words (colour, flavour) to 'or' (color, flavor), for dropping the second 'l' in traveller, and for transposing the last two letters in words such as 'centre' and 'theatre' in the US vernacular. He wasn't consciously using a different spelling to that of the Brits; he just wanted the spelling to match the sound. He also tried to simplify the spellings of other words by dropping the English silent 'e' (imagine to imagin, definite to definit) and 'b' (thumb to thum), but, fortunately, this idea didn't catch on quite as well and was later dropped.

TOP TEN FICTIONAL PARTNERSHIPS

Every Batman needs his Robin...

Hansel and Gretel
Jim Casy and Tom Joad (*The Grapes of Wrath*)
Dante and Virgil (*The Divine Comedy*)
Jeeves and Wooster
Winston Smith and Julia (*1984*)
Lenny and George (*Of Mice and Men*)
Jekyll and Hyde
Frodo Baggins and Samwise Gamgee (*The Lord of the Rings*)
Sherlock Holmes and Dr Watson
Vladimir and Estragon (*Waiting for Godot*)

QUOTE UNQUOTE

*When I get a little money, I buy books; and if any is left,
I buy food and clothes.*
Desiderius Erasmus, Dutch humanist

WRITER WHIMS

Ernest Hemingway stood when he wrote, preferably in a pair of oversized loafers, with the typewriter and the reading board chest-high opposite him.

Robert Frost preferred to write while sitting in an armchair.

Charles Dickens always slept facing towards the North because he thought that it would improve his writing. He also used to touch everything three times for luck.

Lewis Carroll wrote most of his books, including *Alice's Adventures in Wonderland*, while standing up. He composed the tale when sitting down – in a boat with the family of the Dean of Christ Church college, Oxford, including 10-year-old daughter, Alice.

Truman Capote would only ever write on yellow paper.

Balzac believed that in order to write a great book he needed to remain chaste. Every time he spent the night with a woman, he would say to himself: 'There goes another masterpiece.'

Roald Dahl wrote his best-loved works in a specially designated writing hut in his orchard.

French novelist **Colette** didn't just read in bed, she preferred to write there too. To make things all the more comfortable, she invented a 'bed-raft' in her Paris apartment on which she slept, ate, entertained, phoned, read and wrote.

The total floor area, in thousands of square metres, of the British Library building at St Pancras, London

LITERARY PRIZES

The award every writer doesn't want to receive, the Bad Sex in Fiction Award, celebrates just that – the worst examples of sex scenes in contemporary literature. The 2003 prize (presented by the allegedly highly-sexed singer Sting) was awarded to Indian writer Aniruddha Bahal for a scene in *Bunker 13* involving a woman who has a swastika shaven into her pubic hair. Among the nominees were Hollywood director Alan Parker, Conservative politician Iain Duncan Smith and authors Paul Theroux, Paolo Coelho and John Updike.

The prize was launched in 1994 when Philip Hook raised the bar with the following scene in *The Stonebreakers*: 'Their jaws ground in feverish mutual mastication. Saliva and sweat. Sweat and saliva. There was a purposeful shedding of clothing.' Winners receive a box of cigars for their efforts.

QUOTE UNQUOTE

Having to read a footnote resembles having to go downstairs to answer the door while in the midst of making love.
Noël Coward, British dramatist

THE BORROWER

Unpack the books holed up in your attic and you're sure to find the odd 'misplaced' library book or two, but have you ever thought about taking them back? Wary of fines, most hastily return them to the shelves, but not so Ernie Roscouet who, in 2004, returned a book to a library in Malta 42 years too late. Expecting a massive fine or even imprisonment, Roscouet was presented with an altogether different reaction – a cup of tea, as a reward.

WISE WORDS

Literature with a spiritual point

John Bunyan ....*Pilgrim's Progress*
Teresa of Avila ....*The Life of Saint Teresa of Avila By Herself*
Lao Tzu ....*Tao Te Ching*
Prince Siddhartha Gautama ....*The Dhammapada*
Confucius ....*The Analects*
Mother Julian of Norwich ....*Revelations of Divine Love*
Paulo Coelho ....*The Alchemist: A Fable About Following Your Dream*
James Redfield ....*The Celestine Prophecy*
Richard Bach ....*Jonathan Livingston Seagull: A Story*

NAME DROPPERS

First names of writers better known by other names
Lord Byron – George
Colette – Sidonie
Harper Lee – Nelle
Ogden Nash – Frederic
Beatrix Potter – Helen
Rudyard Kipling – Joseph
Salman Rushdie – Ahmed
Virginia Woolf – Adeline

LITERARY PRIZES

The Nobel Prize for Literature takes its name and foundation from Alfred Nobel, brilliant scientist, literary intellectual and philanthropist, who left instructions for the prize categories (chemistry, physics, medicine, literature, peace, economics) in his will.

The first winner was Sully Prud'Homme, the French Poet Laureate, in 1901.

The first British winner was Rudyard Kipling in 1907. He was also the youngest to pick up the prize, receiving it at the age of 42.

The last British nominee to receive the prize was Winston Churchill – he picked it up in 1953 at the age of 79. The oldest winner was also British.

Bertrand Russell accepted the prize in 1950 when he was 78.

William Faulkner's Nobel Prize was awarded a year late – in 1950 – because the committee couldn't make up its mind in time. It was reportedly one of the most difficult decisions in the award's history, as the list also included Hemingway, Steinbeck, Pasternak, Sholokhov, Mauriac, Camus and Winston Churchill.

The only winner to have declined the prize was Jean-Paul Sartre. He refused it in 1964, apparently because he believed Pablo Neruda should have won it.

The first American woman to pick up the award was Pearl Buck. She received it in 1938 at the age of 46.

QUOTE UNQUOTE

A book is a mirror: if an ass peers into it, you can't expect an apostle to look out.
Georg C Lichtenberg, German satirist

LITERARY HOARDERS

Humans have been collecting written knowledge together as long as they have been writing it...

- The earliest-known collection of reading materials – a series of clay tablets – was established in ancient Mesopotamia 5,000 years ago. Archaeologists also uncovered a store of papyrus scrolls from 1300–1200 BC in the ancient Egyptian cities of Amarna and Thebes and thousands of clay tablets in the palace of King Sennacherib, Assyrian ruler from 704–681BC, at Nineveh, his capital city.

- The first private library is attributed to Aristotle. Ancient geographer Strabo reported that Aristotle 'was the first to have put together a collection of books and to have taught the kings in Egypt how to arrange a library'. As a result of his instructions, the first public library was opened in Alexandria in 330 BC under Ptolemy I.

- In the early 500s, Pachomius established a monastery in Egypt at which literacy was compulsory. This subsequently sparked an explosion of learning that saw theological libraries spring up all over the monastic world.

- Theological collections grew side by side with royal libraries. France's national library, the Bibliothèque Nationale de France, began life in 1367 as the Royal Library of Charles V.

- The earliest public library in the UK was associated with London's Guild Hall in 1425. A second opened in Edinburgh, Scotland, in 1580.

- Sir Thomas Bodley rebuilt the Duke of Gloucester's library at Oxford in the late 1500s. It was renamed the Bodleian Library, and today is the second largest in the country, behind the British Library, which was founded in 1759 as part of the British Museum.

- Once British Parliament passed the Public Library Act in 1850, libraries began to spread throughout the nation. Today, 58% of Britons are library members, borrowing some 480 million books a year.

THUMBS UP FROM THE VATICAN

Lew Wallace's *Ben Hur* (1880) was the first piece of fiction ever to be blessed by a pope.

The first recognised formal system of punctuation was developed by the Greek scholar Aristophanes of Byzantium, librarian at Alexandria around 200 BC. His system used a set of three points of varying heights: 'media distinctio', which served the function of a comma (a short pause); 'subdistinctio', which served the function of a colon or semicolon (a longer pause); and 'distinctio', which marked a very long pause (more or less the function of a full stop).

By the first century BC, the only punctuation marks really in use were occasional 'interpuncts' (small vertically centred dots found between words), which the Romans used to indicate the break up of words in formal inscriptions, such as those found on buildings and monuments.

The consistent use of spaces between words didn't appear until 600–800 AD. Manuscripts from this time also used two vertically aligned dots to represent a full stop. One of the dots was later dropped, and the remaining dot served as a comma or colon, depending on whether it was aligned with the top, middle, or base of the lowercase letters.

After the fall of Rome, Western Europe lapsed into illiteracy. The apathy came to an end, however, when English deacon and scholar Alcuin of York established a consistent writing style for use by ninth-century scribes. In it, he introduced the Caroline minuscules, the forerunners of our own lowercase letters; the use of capitals to begin sentences; the use of spaces between words; and the arranging of text into sentences and paragraphs.

Aldus Manutius (1449–1515), the Renaissance typographer and printer later put Alcuin's style into consistent usage. Manutius used a dot – '.' – to indicate a full stop at the end of a sentence and a diagonal slash – '/' – to represent a pause.

The basic form of the question mark – '?' – was developed much later, in sixteenth-century England. It was derived from an abbreviation of the Latin word 'quaestio' ('what') and used a capital 'q' atop a lowercase 'o', which gradually evolved into the mark we use today.

Quotation marks, the apostrophe, the hyphen and the exclamation mark were added in the seventeenth and eighteenth centuries. In 1906, lexicographers Henry Watson Fowler and Francis George Fowler published The King's English, in which they established the current British practice of light punctuation.

THE REWRITE WAS BETTER

Stupid White Pen
Michael Moore launches a blistering attack on
George W Bush's preferred writing utensil.

WRITERS ON WRITING

An author ought to consider himself, not as a gentleman who gives a
private or eleemosynary treat, but rather as one who keeps a public
ordinary, at which all persons are welcome for their money. In the former case, it is well known that the entertainer provides what fare he
pleases; and though this should be very indifferent, and utterly disagreeable to the taste of his company, they must not find any fault;
nay, on the contrary, good breeding forces them outwardly to approve
and to commend whatever is set before them. Now the contrary of
this happens to the master of an ordinary.

Men who pay for what they eat will insist on gratifying their
palates, however nice and whimsical these may prove; and if everything is not agreeable to their taste, will challenge a right to censure,
to abuse, and to d--n [*sic*] their dinner without controul.

Henry Fielding in the Preface to *Tom Jones*

LITERARY LOVE

Romances that blossomed over a book launch or two...

Margaret Drabble and Michael Holroyd
Novelist Margaret Drabble and biographer Michael Holroyd have been husband and wife since the early 1980s.

Sylvia Plath and Ted Hughes
One of the best known literary matches, famous for its tumultuous and destructive edge.

Rimbaud and Verlaine
Two French poets who embarked on a passionate relationship fuelled by absinthe and hashish. After Rimbaud threatened to finish it in 1873, Verlaine shot him and was imprisoned for two years.

Virginia Woolf and Vita Sackville-West
A love affair that provided Woolf with the inspiration for *Orlando*.

Lord Byron and Lady Caroline Lamb
Novelist Lamb is best known for her short but tempestuous relationship with poet Byron. He ended the affair after four months; she termed him 'mad, bad and dangerous to know'.

Simone de Beauvoir and Jean-Paul Sartre
These two influential philosophers and novelists, who were among the first proponents of existentialism, socialism and anti-colonialism, really were a match made in heaven.

Claire Tomalin and Michael Frayn
Biographer and editor Claire Tomalin meets playwright and novelist Michael Frayn, both independent winners of the Whitbread Novel Award. Love, prizes, success follows... What more do you need?

LITERARY BANDWAGONS

McSweeneyites

A coterie of high-selling, high-fashion, post-ironic writers that has recently come begging to the halls of literary history, the McSweeneyites may still have a lot to prove. Spiritually led by American writer Dave Eggers, whose confessional first novel made him more money than he knew what to do with, it numbers Jonathan Safran Foer and British writers Zadie Smith and Nick Hornby among its members. Advocates of what they dub 'casualness' in writing, the McSweeneyites (named after Eggers' publishing firm) have been known to pepper their work with line drawings and visual gimmickry. Vastly successful, youthful and attractive, the McSweeneyites have faced criticism for being too insular and allowing the outlook of the group to stifle the imagination of the individual.

WRITERS ON WRITING

Camerado, this is no book,
Who touches this touches a man,
(Is it night? are we here together alone?)
It is I you hold and who holds you,
I spring from the pages into your arms – decease
    calls me forth
O how your fingers drowse me,
Your breath falls around me like dew, your pulse
    lulls the tympans of my ears,
I feel immerged from head to foot,
Delicious, enough

Walt Whitman, *Leaves of Grass*

POETIC PUZZLERS

My first is in poetry, but never in song
My second's in Ireland, where I do come from
My third is in heat, but never in cold
My fourth is in centre, that which cannot hold
My fifth is in second, and also in still
My whole is a poet whose first name is Bill
Answer on page 153.

MURDER SHE WROTE

When police found the car of 36-year-old Agatha Christie hidden in a clump of bushes a dozen or so miles away from her Berkshire home, on the morning of the 4 December 1926, they suspected first suicide and then murder. But while it seemed that prime suspect Archibald Christie, Agatha's husband, might stand to gain from the death of his wife, he had a pretty solid alibi for the night of her disappearance. Where was he? At a weekend party in Surrey with his mistress, Nancy Neele.

Just 11 days after the author disappeared, a waiter revealed her whereabouts – she had been hiding out in a hotel in Harrogate, Yorkshire, under the assumed name of Teresa Neele. Archibald originally claimed that his wife had lost her memory (no one believed his story, least of all the Surrey police who presented him with a bill for the cost of the search) and it wasn't until after the detective writer's death that the truth finally emerged.

It seems the author had found out about his affair and concocted the plan to scare her husband into leaving his mistress. It didn't work – they were divorced two years later.

FLYING FICTION

The Raven, Edgar Allen Poe
Birdsong, Sebastian Faulks
The Crocodile Bird, Ruth Rendell
Wild Swans, Jung Chang
The Eagle has Landed, Jack Higgins
The Maltese Falcon, Dashiell Hammett
Thorn Birds, Colleen McCullough
To Kill a Mockingbird, Harper Lee
Where Eagles Dare, Alistair MacLean
White Eagles over Serbia, Lawrence Durrell

A LITERARY ROAD TRIP

The world's biggest library is the Library of Congress, Washington DC, USA. It contains 28 million books and has 532 miles of shelving. If you were driving at a constant 70 mph in a car it would take you just under eight hours to pass them all. The British Library in London is the second largest with 18 million books on its shelves.

MAN'S MACHINES

Good or evil, robots have appeared in literature since Homer first wrote of maidens made of gold and the bronze giant Talos in *The Iliad*; here are our top-ten robotic creations...

- The robotic chess-player in Ambrose Bierce's *Moxon's Master* (1894)
- The evil Cyclops intent on zapping the world in HG Well's *The War of the Worlds* (1898)
- The tin woodsman in L Frank Baum's Oz books (1900) – 'If I only had a heart...'
- The Martian robot in John Wyndham's *The Lost Machine* (1932)
- The robotic surgeon in Harl Vincent's *Rex* (1934)
- The robots who discover their roots in Robert Moore Williams' *Robots Return* (1938)
- *The Iron Man*, in the book of the same name by Ted Hughes (1968)
- The perfect-looking, obedient robot replicas conceived to replace women in Ira Levin's *The Stepford Wives* (1972)
- Andrew Martin from *The Bicentennial Man* (1976)
- The fully organic androids produced by genetic engineering in Philip K Dick's *Do Androids Dream of Electric Sheep?* (1968)

THE WRITTEN WORD

Literary figures who have made their way into the English vernacular...

Bowdlerise – to expurgate a book; from British writer Bowdler (1754–1825), expurgator of Shakespeare

Clerihew – a short comic or nonsensical verse; from British writer Edmund Clerihew Bentley (1875–1956)

Dickensian – poor social conditions; from Charles Dickens

Kafkaesque – an oppressive, nightmarish situation; from Czech author Franz Kafka (1883–1924)

Knickerbockers – loose-fitting breeches; from Dietrich Knickerbocker, pseudonym of American author Washington Irving (1783–1859)

Malapropism – the use of a wrong word for comic effect; from Mrs Malaprop, character in the play *The Rivals* by Irish dramatist Richard Brinsley Sheridan (1751–1816)

Masochism – sexual gratification from one's own pain or humiliation; from Austrian novelist Leopold von Sacher-Masoch (1836–95), who described cases of it

Mentor – an experienced or trusted advisor; from Mentor, Odysseus's loyal friend in Homer's *The Odyssey*

Pander – to gratify or indulge a person, desire or weakness; from Pandarus a character in poem *Filostrato* by the Italian author Giovanni Boccaccio (1313–1375)

Sadism – sexual gratification from someone else's pain or humiliation; as described by the French soldier and writer the Marquis de Sade (1740–1814)

Svengali – a person who exercises a controlling or mesmerising influence on another; from the character Svengali in *Trilby* by English artist and writer George du Maurier (1834–1896)

Syphilis – venereal disease; from the character Syphilis in the poem *Syphilis seve morbus Gallicus* by Girolamo Fracastro (1483–1553) who was supposed to be the first to suffer from the disease

Wendy House – a small house-like tent; from the house built around Wendy in *Peter Pan* by JM Barrie (1860–1937)

Zany – comically idiotic; from Zanni, the traditional masked clown in the Italian *commedia dell'arte*

EASY, MY FRIEND WATSON

It's one of the world's most famous catchphrases, but in reality, Sherlock Holmes never once uttered, 'Elementary, my dear Watson' – not in the books that is. The oft-quoted phrase, like Holmes' curved calabash pipe (introduced by actor William Gillette) and deerstalker hat, was a creation of the film adaptation.

Number of signatories on the Déclaration sur le droit à l'insoumission dans la 121
guerre d'Algérie, *a text widely attributed to the French essayist Maurice Blanchot*

SEQUELS BY ANOTHER AUTHOR

Alice's Adventures in Wonderland (Lewis Carroll)
– *Alice through the Needle's Eye* (Gilbert Adair)

Emma (Jane Austen)
– *Aunt Celia* (Jane Gillespie)
– *Emma in Love* (Emma Tennant)
– *Later Days at Highbury* (Joan Austen-Leigh)
– *Perfect Happiness* (Rachel Billington)

Gone with the Wind (Margaret Mitchell)
– *Scarlett* (Alexandra Ripley)
Ripley was picked to write the 'official' sequel by Mitchell

Rebecca (Daphne du Maurier)
– *Mrs de Winter* (Susan Hill)
The cover states: 'Daphne du Maurier would approve'

Great Expectations (Charles Dickens)
– *Magwitch* (Michael Noonan)

Heidi (Johanna Spyri)
– *Heidi Grows Up* (Charles Tritten)
Tritten was the translator of the original *Heidi*

King Lear (Shakespeare)
– *King Lear* (Tate Nahum)
Nahum's version ends with a happy marriage between Cordelia and Edgar

Sense and Sensibility (Jane Austen)
– *The Third Sister* (Julia Barrett)

Pride and Prejudice (Jane Austen)
– *An Unequal Marriage: Pride and Prejudice Twenty Years Later* (Emma Tennant)
– *The Bar Sinister, Pride and Prejudice Continues* (Linda Berdoll)
– *Excessively Diverted: The Sequel to Jane Austen's Pride and Prejudice* (Juliette Shapiro)
– *Lady Catherine's Necklace* (Joan Aiken)
– *Mr Darcy's Daughters* (Elizabeth Aston)
– *Presumption: An Entertainment* (Julia Barrett)
– *Desire and Duty* (Ted Bader and Marilyn Bader)
The couple followed it with *Virtue and Vanity*, another *Pride and Prejudice* sequel

Mansfield Park (Jane Austen)
– *Mansfield Revisited* (Joan Aiken)
– *The Youngest Miss Ward* (Joan Aiken)

Wind in the Willows (Kenneth Grahame)
– *A Fresh Wind in the Willows* (Dixon Scott)
– *The Willows in Winter* (William Horwood)

Wuthering Heights (Emily Brontë)
– *Heathcliff* (Jeffrey Caine)
– *Return to Wuthering Heights* (Anna L'Estrange)
– *The Story of Heathcliff's Journey Back to Wuthering Heights* (Lin Haire-Sargeant)

THE REWRITE WAS BETTER

Oliver Pissed
Born into a workhouse in 1830s England, a difficult life of
crime and grime leaves its mark on Oliver Pissed.

POETIC PUZZLERS

In Oliver Goldsmith's 1766 novel, who was the vicar of Wakefield?
Answer on page 153.

POETIC CRIB

Meter works through recurrent regular stressed and unstressed
syllables. The four standard types of strong and weak stresses (known
as feet) are...

Iambic – light syllable then stressed syllable
The cur – few tolls – the knell – of par – ting day.
Thomas Gray, 'Elegy Written in a Country Churchyard'
Anapestic – two light syllables then stressed syllable
The Assyr – ian came down – like a wolf – on the fold.
Byron, 'The Destruction of Sennacherib'
Trochaic – stressed syllable then light syllable
There they – are, my – fifty – men and – women.
Robert Browning, 'One Word More'
Dactylic – stressed syllable then two light syllables
Eve, with her – basket, was – deep in the – bells and grass.
Ralph Hodgson, 'Eve'.

The **Whitbread Book of the Year** was established in 1971 to celebrate British fiction in five categories: first novel, novel, biography, poetry and children's book. In 2003, the £5,000 cash prizes went to DBC Pierre for *Vernon God Little* (first novel); Mark Haddon for *The Curious Incident of the Dog in the Night-Time* (novel); DJ Taylor for *Orwell: The Life* (biography); Don Paterson for *Landing Light* (poetry); and David Almond for *The Fire-Eaters* (children's book).

The **WH Smith Thumping Good Read Award** has been awarded by customers since 1992 for books more 'accessible' to the public than the high-brow 'literary' choices of the more elite prize crew – that'll be a shortlist of murder mysteries, espionage thrillers and picture books then. In 2003 the award – £5,000 – went to Harlan Coben for his novel *Gone for Good*.

The Arts Council has been doling out the **David Cohen British Literature Prize**, a relatively new entry to the prize circuit, since 1993. Prizes up to a total value of £40,000 are awarded after votes cast by the general public. In 2003, it was jointly awarded to Beryl Bainbridge and Thom Gunn.

The **Forward Poetry Prizes** are awarded annually in three categories: best poetry collection of the year (£10,000), best first collection (£5,000) and best single poem (£1,000). The **TS Eliot Prize**, administered by the Poetry Book Society, gives £5,000 every year to the best new collection of poetry published in the UK or the Republic of Ireland.

The **Orange Prize for Fiction** awards female novelists with a £30,000 grand prize and a bronze figurine known as the 'Bessie'. Helen Dunmore's *A Spell of Winter* was the first winner, in 1996.

Established in 1947 by W Somerset Maugham to enable British authors under the age of 35 to enrich their writing by spending time abroad, the **Somerset Maugham Award** is, perhaps, best known for the time Kingsley Amis won with *Lucky Jim*. Famously unwilling to travel abroad, Amis chose not to take up the offer of a trip and instead used the money to write *I Like It Here*.

The **BBC FOUR Samuel Johnson Prize for Non-fiction** was established in 1998 to reward contemporary non-fiction publishing. The annual prize is worth £30,000 to the winner and £2,500 to the short-listed authors.

Organised by Publishing News, the **British Book Awards** (also known as the 'Nibbies') celebrate the bookselling end of the business with nominations for Publisher of the Year, Chain Bookseller of the Year, Display Creations In-Store Marketing Award,

LITERARY CAMOUFLAGE

Female authors who hid their sex

Acton, Currer and Ellis Bell – Anne, Charlotte and Emily Brontë
The Brontës used these pseudonyms in their first published work – a joint volume of verse entitled *Poems by Currer, Ellis and Acton Bell* – but soon revealed themselves after suspicions that the Bell pennames concealed but one author.

Isak Dinesen – Baroness Karen Christentze Blixen, author of *Out of Africa*

George Eliot – Mary Ann (later Marian) Evans

PD James – Phyllis Dorothy James White

Harper Lee – Nelle Harper Lee

George Sand – Amandine-Aurore Lucille Dupin

Even today female authors hide their sex; JK Rowling's publishers allegedly used her initials on the book cover because they didn't think boys would buy a book by a woman.

WRITERS ON WRITING

Fortune suddenly smiled upon Jo, and dropped a good luck penny in her path. Not a golden penny, exactly, but I doubt if half a million would have given more real happiness then did the little sum that came to her in this wise. Every few weeks she would shut herself up in her room, put on her scribbling suit, and 'fall into a vortex', as she expressed it, writing away at her novel with all her heart and soul, for till that was finished she could find no peace. Her 'scribbling suit' consisted of a black woolen pinafore on which she could wipe her pen at will, and a cap of the same material, adorned with a cheerful red bow, into which she bundled her hair when the decks were cleared for action. This cap was a beacon to the inquiring eyes of her family, who during these periods kept their distance, merely popping in their heads semi-occasionally to ask, with interest, 'Does genius burn, Jo?' They did not always venture even to ask this question, but took an observation of the cap, and judged accordingly. If this expressive article of dress was drawn low upon the forehead, it was a sign that hard work was going on, in exciting moments it was pushed rakishly askew, and when despair seized the author it was plucked wholly off, and cast upon the floor, and cast upon the floor. At such times the intruder silently withdrew, and not until the red bow was seen gaily erect upon the gifted brow, did anyone dare address Jo.

Louisa May Alcott, *Little Women*

Mrs Morland was a very good woman, and wished to see her children everything they ought to be; but her time was so much occupied in lying-in and teaching the little ones, that her elder daughters were inevitably left to shift for themselves; and it was not very wonderful that Catherine, who had by nature nothing heroic about her, should prefer cricket, baseball, riding on horseback, and running about the country at the age of fourteen, to books – or at least books of information – for, provided that nothing like useful knowledge could be gained from them, provided they were all story and no reflection, she had never any objection to books at all. But from fifteen to seventeen she was in training for a heroine; she read all such works as heroines must read to supply their memories with those quotations which are so serviceable and so soothing in the vicissitudes of their eventful lives.

From Pope, she learnt to censure those who
      'bear about the mockery of woe.'
From Gray, that
      'Many a flower is born to blush unseen,
      And waste its fragrance on the desert air.'
From Thompson, that
      –'It is a delightful task
      To teach the young idea how to shoot.'
And from Shakespeare she gained a great store of information – amongst the rest, that
      –'Trifles light as air,
      Are, to the jealous, confirmation strong,
      As proofs of Holy Writ.'
That
      'The poor beetle, which we tread upon,
      In corporal sufferance feels a pang as great
      As when a giant dies'
And that a young woman in love always looks
      – 'like Patience on a monument
      Smiling at Grief.'

So far her improvement was sufficient – and in many other points she came on exceedingly well; for though she could not write sonnets, she brought herself to read them

Jane Austen, *Northanger Abbey*

QUOTE UNQUOTE

Writing is easy. All you do is stare at a blank sheet of paper until drops of blood form on your forehead.
Gene Fowler, US biographer

THE BIG BOOK

The Bible has 66 books, divided into 1,189 chapters consisting of 31,173 verses. Its form was defined by Stephen Langton who split it into chapters around 1228. R Nathan subsequently divided the Old Testament into verses in 1448, and Ropert Stephanus did likewise for the New Testament in 1551.

The Venerable Bede initiated the first Anglo-Saxon translation of the Bible at the end of the seventh century. By the late-thirteenth century, Richard Rolle of Hampole began to translate it into Middle English, closely followed by his more famous counterpart, John Wyclif.

The earliest printed Bible, a 1526 translation by William Tyndale, was reproduced on Johannes Gutenberg's printing press in 1531. Today, the Bible is available in 2,233 of the 2,700 languages spoken in the world.

TRULY MADLY DEEPLY

Literature's greatest lovers...

Antony and Cleopatra
Heathcliff and Cathy
Odysseus and Penelope
Abelard and Héloïse
Tristan and Isolde
Romeo and Juliet
Lady Chatterley and Mellors
Jane Eyre and Mr Rochester
Anna Karenina and Alexei Vronski

WRITERS ON READING

Books, books, books!
I had found the secret of a garret-room
Piled high with cases in my father's name;
Piled high, packed large,— where, creeping in and out
Among the giant fossils of my past,
Like some small nimble mouse between the ribs
Of a mastodon, I nibbled here and there
At this or that box, pulling through the gap,
In heats of terror, haste, victorious joy,
The first book first. And how I felt it beat
Under my pillow, in the morning's dark,
An hour before the sun would let me read!
My books!

Elizabeth Barrett Browning, *Aurora Leigh*

PERFECT WORLDS

Sir Thomas More first coined the term 'utopia' (a pun meaning both 'good land' and 'nowhere land' in Greek) for his 1515 work. Generations of authors have since offered their own fantastic takes on both utopia and dystopia…

1984 – George Orwell

The Book of the New Moral World – Robert Owen
Owen founded the community of New Harmony, Indiana, but it failed in 1831, as did most of his experiments in utopian socialism.

Brave New World – Aldous Huxley

Gormenghast – Mervyn Peake

Gulliver's Travels – Jonathan Swift
The island of the Houyhnhnms is proffered as the world's most perfect society, as opposed to the manlike yahoos.

Lost Horizon – James Hilton
It marked the first use of the term 'Shangri-la' to describe a hidden paradise

Riddley Walker – Russell Hoban

The Time Machine – HG Wells

Walden Two – BF Skinner
Skinner believed that humans are a product of their conditioning, so children in his Utopia are raised and educated in a manner that many critics have compared to brainwashing.

QUOTE UNQUOTE

If you can't annoy somebody, there's little point in writing.
Kingsley Amis, British novelist

WHAT A BIND

It all makes perfectly logical sense now, but there was a time when locating a book on the bookshelf was rendered even more difficult by the absence of markings of any kind. The earliest printed books didn't show the title, author or any kind of design on their covers and, as a result, were shelved backwards with the spine at the back of the shelf and the pages facing out. Books were also sold unbound in 'quires' (gatherings of printed sheets), which meant that if you wanted a bound book, you had to buy the quires from the publisher and take them to your nearest bookbinder for binding in your choice (and price) of material.

LESS IS MORE

A short history of the short story...

Up until the fourteenth century, short stories were mainly used to convey religious morals. With Boccaccio's *The Decameron* and Chaucer's *Canterbury Tales,* the shift moved from the sacred to the profane by focusing on human folly instead.

The English short story changed from verse into prose in the fifteenth century, but it didn't really begin to emerge as a form until the nineteenth century when it took off among American writers including Nathaniel Hawthorne and Edgar Allan Poe.

In the UK, such writers as Thomas Hardy mastered the genre: his *Wessex Tales* (1888) was the first successful short story by a British author.

Short stories went from strength to strength in the twentieth century, partly because the rise in literary magazines and journals created a market for the genre.

The genre has suffered a bit of a decline in recent years. At least enough for writer Margaret Wilkinson to launch the *Save our Short Story* campaign in 2002. Check out their website on www.saveourshortstory.org.uk to join the fight and subscribe to the *Endangered Species* online anthology of stories by both known and new writers.

JOINING THE LIBRARY

Joining the library and borrowing books may be free, but it takes a bit of organisation to fill out the application card with all the necessary documents in hand. Here's what you'll need...

- proof of address (a bill less than three months old, a pension or benefit book)
- proof of signature (a credit card or passport)

Once you've joined you can borrow from any of the city or borough's libraries and return loans to any branch. Children aged ten and under may borrow up to seven items; those aged 11 and over may borrow up to ten items.

MOONSHINE

The moons of all the planets are named after Greek gods, except those of Uranus. In this case characters in Shakespeare plays and Alexander Pope's *The Rape of the Lock* are the inspiration. Uranus has five larger moons (Miranda, Ariel, Umbriel, Titania and Oberon), 11 smaller moons (Cordelia, Ophelia, Bianca, Cressida, Desdemona, Juliet, Portia, Rosalind, Belinda, Puck and one still to be named) and five irregular moons (Caliban, Sycorax, Setebos, Stephano and Prospero).

One tends to picture polar explorers as unwashed fellows slogging wordlessly through the snow on half-rations of pemmican hoosh, and so they often were. But before many of those slogs began, the men had to overwinter at surprisingly civilized base camps, of which Cape Evans, the cosy little Antarctic hut where Scott and his twenty-four men spent the winter of 1911, was far and away the most highbrow. Three nights a week after dinner – which on special occasions included seal consommé and stewed penguin breast – Scott convened sessions of what he called the Universitas Antartica. Topics for discussion included the future of aviation, the art of Japan, and the parasitology of fish. On non-Universitas evenings, the men listened to Caruso on their gramophone, wrote poetry, painted watercolors, or read books from the Odd Shelves some of them had imported 14,000 miles. Scott himself brought a selection of Russian and Polish novels. Captain Lawrence Edward Grace Oates, an Old Etonian who was described by one of the seamen as a 'gentleman, quite a gentleman, and always a gentleman', brought all five volumes of Charles James Napier's Peninsular War, an epic study of the Napoleonic campaigns in Iberia. Edward Wilson, the chief of the scientific staff... brought the complete works of Tennyson. After reading "In Memoriam", he wrote in his diary that he had "been realising what a perfect piece of faith and hope and religion it is, [and it] makes me feel that if the end comes to me here or hereabout... all will be as it is meant to be." Wilson's diary entry could not have been more prescient.

Anne Fadiman, *Ex Libris, Confessions of a Common Reader*

POETIC CRIB

Simile – comparison between two distinctly different things marked by 'like' or 'as': 'my love is like a red, red rose' (Robert Burns)

Metaphor – application of a distinctly different type of thing without asserting a comparison: 'My love is a red, red rose'

Mixed metaphor – combination of two diverse metaphoric vehicles: 'To take arms against a sea of trouble/ And by opposing end them' (Shakespeare, *Hamlet*)

Dead metaphor – metaphors so overused that we are no longer aware of the difference: 'leg of a table', 'heart of the matter'

Metonymy (Greek for a change of name) – application of one common term for another: the 'Crown' (for the Monarch)

Synecdoche (Greek for taking together) – using a part of something to signify a whole: a 'hundred sails' (for ships)

WANTON HUSSIES

Feisty females and genuine jezebels before Jilly Cooper had a go…

Catherine Earnshaw – *Wuthering Heights*, Emily Brontë (1847)
Willful, romantic and incredibly obsessive, our heroine's passion for Heathcliff becomes so strong that at one point she cries out, 'I am Heathcliff!'

Emma Bovary – *Madame Bovary*, Gustave Flaubert (1857)
Emma embarks on a series of unhappy adulterous affairs before finishing it all off with a bottle of poison. If only she hadn't read so much romantic fiction.

Fanny Hill – *Fanny Hill, Memoirs of a Woman of Pleasure*, John Cleland (1749)
Cleland's sexy parody of Samuel Richardson's Pamela is ranked with *Lady Chatterley's Lover* as one of the frankest treatments of sexuality in English literature.

Lady Chatterley – *Lady Chatterley's Lover*, DH Lawrence (1928)
Lawrence's character is the quintessential literary bad girl.

Molly Bloom – *Ulysses*, James Joyce (1922)
The randy wife of Leopold, Molly has a whale of a time while Leopold is wandering around Dublin.

Moll Flanders – *Moll Flanders*, Daniel Defoe, (1722)
Ms Flanders comes through her dramatic misadventures just about morally unscathed.

Carmen – *Carmen*, Prosper Merimee (1837)
Opera's most famous femme fatale. Provocative, daring and wilful, Carmen is bound to no man, except to her discarded lover Don Jose, who stabs her to death during the dramatic bullfight denouement.

Lady Macbeth – *Macbeth*, William Shakespeare (1606)
Frenzied hand washing cannot wash away this woman's murderous ambitions.

Gigi – *Gigi*, Colette (1943)
This sixteen-year-old coquette, destined to be the mistress of a French roué, upsets her family's well laid plans and Parisien society's expectations by refusing to give it away and manoeuvring her man into marriage.

Myra – *Myra Breckinridge*, Gore Vidal (1968)
Dominatrix drama teacher Myra sets out to control her Hollywood wannabe students with classic put-down lines. Responsible for the immortal, 'I'm afraid, Rusty, that you've been somewhat oversold on the campus. Poor Mary-Ann. That's a boy's equipment.' Myra is eventually unmasked herself, as a transexual who's undergone gender reassignment surgery. Considered pornographic when published in 1968, Gore Vidal's satirical novel became an instant best seller.

War and Peas
An epic study of the Napoleonic war and a celebration
of the small vegetable that resolved it.

WHAT'S WHAT IN A BOOK

The printer begins with a large sheet; if the sheet is folded once so as to form two 'leaves' of four pages, the book is a **folio** (Latin for leaf); a sheet folded twice into four 'leaves' is a **quarto**; a sheet folded three times into eight leaves is an **octavo** (the most frequently used size in modern printing). In a **duodecimo** volume, a sheet is folded to make 12 leaves.

As the book is open in front of you, the page on the right is called a **recto,** and the page on the left a **verso.**

The **colophon** in older books was a note at the end stating such facts as the title, author, printer and date of issue. In modern books the colophon is ordinarily in the front, on the title page.

Incunabula (pl. incunables), the term given to books printed before 1500, derives from the Latin word for 'swaddling clothes'. It describes the 'infancy' of books published before the invention of the Gutenberg Press.

The word 'edition' now designates the total copies of a book that are printed from the same setting of type. A **variorum** edition designates either an edition of work that lists all the textual variants in an author's manuscripts and printed revisions, or an edition that includes a selection of annotations and commentaries on the text by earlier editors and critics.

'What were you doing behind the curtain?' he asked.

'I was reading.'

'Show the book.'

I returned to the window and fetched it thence.

'You have no business to take our books; you are a dependent, mama says; you have no money; your father left you none; you ought to beg, and not to live here with gentlemen's children like us, and eat the same meals we do, and wear clothes at our mama's expense. Now, I'll teach you to rummage my bookshelves: for they ARE mine; all the house belongs to me, or will do in a few years. Go and stand by the door, out of the way of the mirror and the windows.'

I did so, not at first aware what was his intention; but when I saw him lift and poise the book and stand in act to hurl it, I instinctively started aside with a cry of alarm: not soon enough, however; the volume was flung, it hit me, and I fell, striking my head against the door and cutting it. The cut bled, the pain was sharp: my terror had passed its climax; other feelings succeeded.

'Wicked and cruel boy!' I said. 'You are like a murderer – you are like a slave-driver – you are like the Roman emperors!'

Charlotte Brontë, *Jane Eyre*

CREATIVE COCK-UPS

In 1889, the editor of the *San Francisco Examiner*, refused to publish the work of Rudyard Kipling with the words: 'I'm sorry Mr Kipling, but you just don't know how to use the English language. This isn't a kindergarten for amateur writers.' Eight years later, Kipling was awarded the Nobel Prize for Literature.

COULD HAVE BEEN CALLED?

As You Like It – Like You Enjoy It
Catch-22 – Trap XXII
The Cat in the Hat – The Feline in the Cap
The God of Small Things – The Deity of Tiny Objects
Great Expectations – Huge Hopes
The Green Mile – The Emerald Kilometre
Little Women – Mini Females
The Lord of the Rings – The God of the Bands
The Old Man and the Sea – The OAP and the Ocean
The Time Machine – The Occasion Contraption
100 Years of Solitude – Ten Decades of Loneliness

WHO BORROWED WHAT

Each year Public Lending Right releases data which shows which authors and books have proved most popular in the nation's libraries; here are the figures by genre for July 2002 to June 2003...

Cookery
Delia's How to Cook Book Three (Delia Smith, 2001)

Sport Biography
My Autobiography: Unless I'm Very Much Mistaken (Murray Walker, 2002)

Performing Arts/ TV
Richard and Judy: the Autobiography (Richard Madeley and Judy Finnigan, 2002)

Travel/Holiday Guide
The Rough Guide to Spain (Mark Ellingham and John Fisher, 2001)

Travel Book
Notes from a Big Country (Bill Bryson, 1998)

Performing Arts
Michael Palin: a Biography (Jonathan Margolis, 1998)

Historical Biography/ Autobiography
Wild Swans: Three Daughters of China (Jung Chang, 1991)

Adult Poetry
The Nation's Favourite Comic Poems: A Selection of Humorous Verse (Edited by Griff Rhys Jones, 1998)

STRANGE LIBRARY EXHIBITS

People leave the funniest things...

Charles Dickens' candleholder and pet raven (stuffed), Free Library of Philadelphia

Guy Fawkes' gunpowder, British Library

Jeremy Bentham's embalmed corpse (with wax head), University College London

A nineteenth-century Feng Shui Compass; a pencil made by Henry David Thoreau; two teeth of a giant 'the size of a fist'; a sixth-century BC Babylonian cylinder from the reign of Nebuchadnezzar; an eighteenth-century recipe *To Dissolve a Cancer in the Breast*; Nathaniel Hawthorne's passport; pieces of Confederate reconnaissance balloons made from ladies' dress silk; a handbill announcing the abdication of Tsar Nicholas II; and a 'Gay Monopoly' game, New York Public Library

Roald Amundsen sledge from the Antarctica, Australian State Library

POETIC PUZZLERS

Name the poet and poem from these famous lines...

1. A snake came to my water-trough
2. Bent double, like old beggars under sacks
3. Do not go gentle into that good night
4. Earth hath not anything to show more fair
5. How do I love thee? Let me count the ways
6. I met a traveller from an antique land
7. Macavity's a mystery cat: he's called the hidden paw
8. O my love's like a red, red rose
9. Quinquireme of Ninevah from distant Ophir
10. Season of mists and mellow fruitfulness
11. The curfew tolls the knell of parting day
12. Tyger! Tyger! burning bright
13. What is this life if, full of care

Answer on page 153.

LITERARY CLUBS OF OLD LONDON

The Kit-Cat Club (est. 1700)
This club's earliest meetings were held in a tavern on Chancery Lane kept by Christopher Cat (hence the name). One of the club's customs was to toast the era's beauties in verse, which were afterwards engraved on the club glasses. The Earl of Halifax and Sir Samuel Garth were the most prolific contributors to the club's literature, being responsible for 13 toasts between them.

The Blue Stocking Club (est. 1925)
This women's club was founded by Elizabeth Robinson, wife of Edward Montagu as a 'discussion party', which saw such illustrious guests as Horace Walpole, Dr Johnson, Burke, Garrick and other late eighteenth-century literati.

The (Literary) Club (est. 1764)
This popular club boasted members that included Dr Johnson (hence it's other title, Dr Johnson's Club), Edward Burke, Oliver Goldsmith and, later, Tennyson, Gladstone and Lord Salisbury. Its membership was limited to 40. Entry was decided by an anonymous vote which included the 'one black ball will exclude' rule popular among clubs over the ages.

Number of novels, including Ragged Dick and Phil the Fiddler written in the late 1800s by Horatio Alger, a minister fired for 'misconduct with choirboys'

They went, the Ghost and Scrooge, across the hall, to a door at the back of the house. It opened before them, and disclosed a long, bare, melancholy room, made barer still by lines of plain deal forms and desks. At one of these a lonely boy was reading near a feeble fire; and Scrooge sat down upon a form, and wept to see his poor forgotten self as he used to be...

The Spirit touched him on the arm, and pointed to his younger self, intent upon his reading. Suddenly a man, in foreign garments: wonderfully real and distinct to look at: stood outside the window, with an axe stuck in his belt, and leading by the bridle an ass laden with wood.

`Why, it's Ali Baba.' Scrooge exclaimed in ecstasy. 'It's dear old honest Ali Baba. Yes, yes, I know. One Christmas time, when yonder solitary child was left here all alone, he did come, for the first time, just like that. Poor boy. And Valentine,' said Scrooge,' and his wild brother, Orson; there they go. And what's his name, who was put down in his drawers, asleep, at the Gate of Damascus; don't you see him. And the Sultan's Groom turned upside down by the Genii; there he is upon his head. Serve him right. I'm glad of it. What business had he to be married to the Princess.'

To hear Scrooge expending all the earnestness of his nature on such subjects, in a most extraordinary voice between laughing and crying; and to see his heightened and excited face; would have been a surprise to his business friends in the city, indeed.

'There's the Parrot.' cried Scrooge. 'Green body and yellow tail, with a thing like a lettuce growing out of the top of his head; there he is. Poor Robin Crusoe, he called him, when he came home again after sailing round the island. 'Poor Robin Crusoe, where have you been, Robin Crusoe.' The man thought he was dreaming, but he wasn't. It was the Parrot, you know. There goes Friday, running for his life to the little creek. Halloa. Hoop. Hallo.'

Then, with a rapidity of transition very foreign to his usual character, he said, in pity for his former self, 'Poor boy.' and cried again.

'I wish,' Scrooge muttered, putting his hand in his pocket, and looking about him, after drying his eyes with his cuff: 'but it's too late now.'

'What is the matter.' asked the Spirit.

'Nothing,' said Scrooge. 'Nothing. There was a boy singing a Christmas Carol at my door last night. I should like to have given him something: that's all.'

Charles Dickens,
Christmas Carol

NOVELTY POP

Celebrity meets children's literature...

Madonna – *The English Roses* (2003)
Prince Charles – *The Old Man of Lochnagar* (1980)
Sarah Ferguson – *Budgie the Helicopter* (1989)
Bill Cosby – *The Meanest Thing to Say* (1997)
Jamie Lee Curtis – *Today I Feel Silly and Other Moods that Make
My Day* (1998), *Tell Me Again About the Night I Was Born* (1999),
When I Was Little: A Four-Year-Old's Memoir of her Youth (1995)
and Where Do Balloons Go? An Uplifting Mystery (2000)
Mary Chapin Carpenter – *Halley Came to Jackson* (1990)
Jimmy Carter – *The Little Baby Snoogle-Fleejer* (1995)
Sophie Dahl – *The Man With the Dancing Eyes* (2003)

QUOTE UNQUOTE

Reading is like permitting a man to talk a long time,
and refusing you the right to answer.
Ed Howe, US journalist and writer

ON HER MAJESTY'S SEQUEL SERVICE

Absurd plots, sexist dialogue and dirty villains: when Ian Fleming's
Bond charmed his way onto the page, the nation was hooked and
Hollywood followed soon after. But when Fleming died in 1964,
someone had to take over the literary reins...

Kingsley Amis (under the pseudonym Robert Markham):
Colonel Sun (1968)

John Gardner (the official Bond sequel writer): *Licence Renewed*
(1981), *For Special Services* (1982), *Icebreaker* (1983), *Role of
Honour* (1984), *Nobody Lives Forever* (1986), *No Deals, Mr Bond*
(1987), *Scorpius* (1987), *Win Lose or Die* (1989), *Licence to Kill*
(1989), *Brokenclaw* (1990), *The Man From Barbarossa* (1991),
Death is Forever (1992), *Never Send Flowers* (1993), *SeaFire*
(1994), *Golden Eye* (1995), *Cold* (1996)

Raymond Benson: *Zero Minus Ten* (1997), *Tomorrow Never Dies*
(1997), *The Facts of Death* (1998), *High Time to Kill* (1999),
The World is not Enough (1999), *Doubleshot* (2000), *Never Dream
of Dying* (2001), *The Man with the Red Tattoo* (2002),
Die Another Day (2002)

I WILL GO TO THE BALL

A favourite fairytale character of young girls all over the world, Cinderella has appeared in a variety of guises...

- In China, she's known as Yeh-Shen; in the Algonquin Indians of North America as the Rough-Face Girl; and in parts of Africa as Chinye and Nyasha. Scholars disagree about the exact number of variations that exist, but it is estimated to be somewhere between 340 and 3,000.

- The earliest known version originated in China. Recorded by Tuan Ch'eng-shih in the middle of the ninth century, it centres around the beautiful Yeh-Shen who is relegated to the function of maid after her father remarries. In this cautionary tale, the stepmother and evil stepsister are stoned to death for their cruelty.

- The British put a slight twist on the story in *Tattercoats*. This moral parable has the evil stepmother replaced by a loveless grandfather.

- The Grimm brothers retold an even less forgiving version with Aschenputtel ('Ash Girl'). In the Grimm version, the stepsisters are left permanently blinded after their eyes have been pecked out by birds.

- In 1697, French author Charles Perrault published *Contes de ma Mere l'Oye* ('Tales of Mother Goose'). It included the Cinderella story that was later immortalised by Walt Disney. However, in Perrault's original tale, Cinderella's slippers were made out of fur. The story was changed in the 1600s by a translator who confused *vair*, French for 'fur', with *verre*, French for 'glass'.

BOOKSHOP STORIES

An incentive by the British government to encourage the public back to library borrowing got out of hand when they proposed an entrepreneurial new scheme in 2004. Rather than win British readers over with the 'borrow it, it's free' line, they chose instead to give libraries the opportunity to sell their own books. The new scheme will see some 4,700 libraries rent space out to book chains such as Waterstone's, Blackwell's and Dillons in the hope that people seeking to buy books will also be tempted to borrow other works. As JG Ballard put it succinctly: 'It is the equivalent of putting a private drugs firm in the lobby of a hospital and saying to people use this service you have to pay for, not the one which is provided free by the NHS.'

QUOTE UNQUOTE

*Literature is mostly about sex and not much about
having children; and life is the other way around.*
David Lodge, British novelist and academic

WRITERS ON WRITING

This island betrays its own people in the mere act of existing,' he
wrote, and then he crumpled the sheet of paper and flung it into the
corner of the room. This would never do; why could he not write
like a writer of histories? Why could he not write without passion?
Without anger? Without the sense of betrayal and oppression? He
picked up the sheet, already bent at the corners, that he had written
first. It was the title page: 'The New History of Cephallonia'. He
crossed out the first two words and substituted 'A Personal'. Now
he could forget about leaving out the loaded adjectives and the
ancient historical grudges, now he could be vitriolic about the
Romans, the Normans, the Venetians, the Turks, the British, and
even the islanders themselves...

The learned doctor leaned back and read through what he had
just written. It seemed really very poetic to him. He read it through
again and relished some of the phrases. In the margin he wrote,
'Remember, all Cephallonians are poets. Where can I mention this?'
Louis de Bernières, *Captain Corelli's Mandolin*

BOOK CLUB FAVOURITES

Every year Reading Group Choices announce the most read books
of the previous year in book clubs across the US. Here are the top
picks from 2003:

The Secret Life of Bees, Sue Monk Kidd

The Da Vinci Code, Dan Brown

The Red Tent, Anita Diamant

Seabiscuit: An American Legend, Laura Hillenbrand

Life of Pi, Yann Martel

Girl with a Pearl Earring, Tracy Chevalier

Peace Like a River, Leif Enger

Bel Canto, Ann Patchett

The Lovely Bones, Alice Sebold

Empire Falls, Richard Russo

WHEN EDITORS GET IT WRONG

When Andre Bernard was researching rejection letters for *Rotten Rejections: The Letters that Publishers Wish They'd Never Sent*, he came across some howlers....

'The author of this book is beyond psychiatric help.'
Crash by J G Ballard

'This will set publishing back 25 years.'
The Deer Park by Norman Mailer

'Do you realize, young woman, that you're the first American writer ever to poke fun at sex.'
Gentlemen Prefer Blondes by Anita Loos

'The girl doesn't, it seems to me, have a special perception or feeling which would lift that book above the "curiosity" level.'
The Diary of Anne Frank

'A long, dull novel about an artist.'
Lust for Life by Irving Stone

'The grand defect of the work, I think, as a work of art is the low-mindedness and vulgarity of the chief actors. There is hardly a "lady" or "gentleman" amongst them.'
Barchester Towers by Anthony Trollope

'We are not interested in science fiction which deals with negative utopias. They do not sell.'
Carrie by Stephen King

'I haven't really the foggiest idea about what the man is trying to say... Apparently the author intends it to be funny – possibly even satire – but it is really not funny on any intellectual level... From your long publishing experience you will know that it is less disastrous to turn down a work of genius than to turn down talented mediocrities.'
Catch-22 by Joseph Heller

'You're welcome to le Carré – he hasn't got any future.'
The Spy who Came in from the Cold by John le Carré

'It is impossible to sell animal stories in the USA'
Animal Farm by George Orwell

'My dear sir, I have read your manuscript. Oh, my dear sir.'
Lady Windermere's Fan by Oscar Wilde

'Overwhelmingly nauseating, even to an enlightened Freudian... The whole thing is an unsure cross between hideous reality and improbable fantasy. It often becomes a wild neurotic daydream... I recommend that it be buried under a stone for a thousand years.'
Lolita by Vladimir Nabokov

THE REWRITE WAS BETTER

A Short History of Nearly Every String
From primordial nothingness to this very moment,
Bill Bryson records the evolution of string.

POETIC PUZZLERS

In John Fowles' novel, who is the French lieutenant's woman?
Answer on page 153.

BOOKS TO BRAWL TO

Among the Thugs, Bill Buford (2001)
*The Bad Guys Won! A Season of Brawling, Bimbo Chasing, and
Championship Baseball with Straw, Doc, Mookie, Nails, the Kid,
and the Rest of the 1986 Mets*, Jeff Pearlman (2004)
The Bear, William Faulkner (1942)
Bloody Casuals: Diary of a Football Hooligan, Jay Allan (1989)
Fat City, Leonard Gardner (1996)
Fight Club, Chuck Palahniuk (1996)
Glue, by Irvine Welsh (2001)
The Illiad, Homer
Homer describes every blow struck by every soldier...
Raging Bull: My Story, Jake La Motta (1997)
Reservoir Dogs, Quentin Tarantino (2000)
Snatch: The Shooting Script, Guy Ritchie (2001)
The Three Musketeers, Alexandre Dumas (1844)
A Violent Life, Pier Paolo Pasolini (1996)

Ripped-off titles

Of Mice and Men (John Steinbeck, 1937)
Of Mycenae and Men (a BBC2 sitcom starring Diana Dors broadcast in March 1979)

Who's afraid of Virginia Woolf? (Edward Albee, 1962)
Me, I'm afraid of Virginia Woolf (The first of Alan Bennett's *Six Plays*, broadcast on ITV in December 1978)

Walden, or Life in the Woods (Henry David Thoreau, 1854)
Walden Two (Burrhus Frederik Skinner, 1948)

Pamela, or Virtue Rewarded (Samuel Richardson, 1740)
Shamela Andrews, An Apology for the Life of Mrs.
(Henry Fielding, 1741) Although Fielding published the parody under a pseudonym, Richardson was convinced the work was Fielding's and never forgave him.

Portrait of the Artist as a Young Man (James Joyce, 1914)
Portrait of the Artist as a Young Dog (Dylan Thomas, 1920)

The Silmarillion (JRR Tolkien, 1977)
The Sellamillion: The Disappointing 'Other' Book
(ARRR Roberts, 2004)

Eats, Shoots & Leaves: The Zero Tolerance Approach to Punctuation
(Lynne Truss, 2003)
Eats, Shites and Leaves: Crap English and How to Use it
(A Parody, 2004)

Schott's Original Miscellany (Ben Schott, 2003)
Shite's Unoriginal Miscellany (A Parody, 2003)

Harry Potter books, JK Rowling
Barry Trotter and the Shameless Parody (Michael Gerber, 2002)
'utterly unauthorized and blazenly exploitative' reads the dust jacket
Barry Trotter and the Unnecessary Sequel (Michael Gerber, 2003)
'the book nobody has been waiting for' the author continues
Barry Trotter and the Dead Horse (Michael Gerber, 2004)

Lord of the Rings (JRR Tolkien, 1954–1955)
Bored of the Rings (Harvard National Lampoon, 1969)

QUOTE UNQUOTE

There is no such thing as a moral or immoral book; books are well written or badly written.
Oscar Wilde, British playwright

BOOK IN BOOK READING

Books in which protagonists read...

David Copperfield, Charles Dickens

Gone with the Wind, Margaret Mitchell.
Melanie reads Dickens aloud to a group of women tensely awaiting word of their men out on a vigilante mission.

Jane Eyre, Charlotte Brontë

Madame Bovary, Gustave Flaubert
The potentially misleading influence of romantic fiction is brought to life in Flaubert's Emma Bovary.

Swallows and Amazons, Arthur Ransome
All the children, but especially the sensitive protagonist Titty Walker, adore *Robinson Crusoe*.

The Never Ending Story, Stephen B Grant

To Kill a Mockingbird, Harper Lee
Jem is forced to read each day to a dying old woman who is trying to break her addiction to morphine.

Northanger Abbey, Jane Austen
Austen charts a young woman's reading habits and the impact on her character.

A BARDLESS WORLD

Unimaginable it may seem, but we could now have a world without Shakespeare. The Bard's genius was little appreciated during his lifetime and as the years passed, his work was first criticised and then forgotten. Seven years after his death in 1616, two actors in his company, John Heminge and Henry Condell, resurrected the original copies and scratched together the funds to publish them in one authoritative volume: the first folio. History has proved their enthusiasm justified, even though it wasn't until 1769, after the first Stratford Festival, that 'Bardolatry' really took off.

Number of personal letters written by Ted Hughes to his friend and critic 143
Keith Sagar over a 30-year period

A work that aspires, however humbly, to the condition of art should carry its justification in every line. And art itself may be defined as a single-minded attempt to render the highest kind of justice to the visible universe, by bringing to light the truth, manifold and one, underlying its every aspect. It is an attempt to find in its forms, in its colors, in its light, in its shadows, in the aspects of matter and in the facts of life what of each is fundamental, what is enduring and essential-- their one illuminating and convincing quality – the very truth of their existence. The artist, then, like the thinker or the scientist, seeks the truth and makes his appeal. Impressed by the aspect of the world the thinker plunges into ideas, the scientist into facts – whence, presently, emerging they make their appeal to those qualities of our being that fit us best for the hazardous enterprise of living. They speak authoritatively to our common-sense, to our intelligence, to our desire of peace or to our desire of unrest; not seldom to our prejudices, sometimes to our fears, often to our egoism – but always to our credulity. And their words are heard with reverence, for their concern is with weighty matters: with the cultivation of our minds and the proper care of our bodies, with the attainment of our ambitions, with the perfection of the means and the glorification of our precious aims.

It is otherwise with the artist...

Art is long and life is short, and success is very far off. And thus, doubtful of strength to travel so far, we talk a little about the aim – the aim of art, which, like life itself, is inspiring, difficult – obscured by mists. It is not in the clear logic of a triumphant conclusion; it is not in the unveiling of one of those heartless secrets which are called the Laws of Nature. It is not less great, but only more difficult.

Joseph Conrad in the Preface to
The Nigger of the 'Narcissus'

DUMBING DOWN

The Penguin 'Good Booking' promotion sees the well-reputed publishing house take something of a more low-brow approach to book marketing. In order to 'make reading more attractive to young men', they launched a new campaign in 2004 to 'make young men who read more attractive to women'. Male readers are encouraged to visit the Good Booking website (www.goodbooking.com), which rates books using icons such as 'sex', 'nudity', 'kinky sex', 'greed', 'drugs', 'fast cars' (that eternal winner) – and, presumably, 'pull factor'. That's reverse psychology for you.

ALL-TIME TOP TEN BEST-SELLERS

1. *The Bible* (c.1451–5)
   2.5 billion copies sold in 2,233 languages and dialects
2. *Quotations from the Works of Mao Tse-tung* (1966)
   800 million; formerly known as *The Red Book*
3. *The Lord of the Rings,* JRR Tolkien (1954–55)
   More than 100 million
4. *American Spelling Book,* Noah Webster (1783)
   100 million
5. *The Guinness Book of Records* (now *Guinness World Records,* 1955)
   More than 90 million
6. *World Almanac* (1868)
   70 million
7. *The McGuffey Readers*, William Holmes McGuffey (1836)
   60 million
8. *The Common Sense Book of Baby and Child Care,*
   Benjamin Spock (1946)
   More than 50 million
9. *A Message to Garcia*, Elbert Hubbard (1899)
   Up to 40 million
10. *Valley of the Dolls*, Jacqueline Susann (1966)
    More than 30 million

ADOPT A BOOK

With many of the British Library's 150 million volumes deteriorating with age and use, the library asked the British public in 2004 to 'adopt a book and save it for a nation'. For £25, donors sponsor a book and receive a certificate of adoption; for £75, a book and a library tour for two; and for £1,000 the opportunity of picking a book of their choice. Bibliophiles should head to www.bl.uk/adoptabook to find out more – but remember, books are for life, not just for Christmas.

LITERARY LINGOS

Nerd – Coined by Dr Seuss in *If I Ran the Zoo* (1950)

Robot – First appeared in Czech playwright Karl Capek's *RUR* (1920), as a derivation of the Czech word for work (robota)

Heavy metal – Penned by William Burroughs in *The Naked Lunch* (1959)

Number of writers featured in the Norton anthology, Jewish American 145
Literature *(2000)*

LITERARY PAY OFFS

When celebrated British novelist Fay Weldon brokered a deal in 2001 with Italian jewellery maker Bulgari to plug their products in her novel appropriately entitled *The Bulgari Collection*, the literary world was up in arms. But Weldon wasn't the last novelist to accept cash for product placement in fiction. In 2004, Ford paid British novelist Carole Matthews an undisclosed (but allegedly five-digit) sum in return for featuring the Ford Fiesta in her next two novels. But Matthews dismissed claims it was a sell out: 'Wherever my heroine is driving a car, it will now be a Ford Fiesta,' she told the BBC's World Business Report. 'That's the only thing they've asked me to do, they've placed no other constraints on my writing at all.'

QUOTE UNQUOTE

In the case of good books, the point is not how many of them you can get through, but rather how many can get through to you.
Mortimer Adler, US philosopher and author

A BRIEF HISTORY OF BRAILLE

Parisian Louis Braille invented the Braille reading system nearly 200 years ago at the age of 15 when attending the Royal Institution for Blind Youth.

French army captain, Charles Barbier de la Serre, had invented the basic technique of using raised dots for tactile writing and reading to allow soldiers to compose and read messages at night without light. Barbier presented his system (Sonography) to the Institution for Blind Youth, hoping that it would be officially adopted there. Braille discovered both the potential of the basic idea and the shortcomings and within three years had developed the system that we know today as Braille, which employs a six-dot 'cell', or character based on normal spelling.

Each Braille cell is made up of six dot positions, which are arranged in a rectangle comprising two columns of three dots. A dot may be raised at any of the six positions, and in any combination. Counting the space – where no dots are raised – there are 64 combinations.

Louis Braille published the first Braille book in 1829. In 1837, he added symbols for maths and music. Today, in virtually every language around the world, the code named after Louis Braille is the standard form of writing and reading used by blind people.

THE REWRITE WAS BETTER

Mild Swans

LITERARY FESTIVALS

The best of the rest in the UK

The Althorp Literary Festival
June, www.althorp.com
A new festival launched by
Countess Spencer in 2004.

**The Clerkenwell Literary
Festival** *July*
www.clerkenwelllitfest.org
Literature meets comedy, art
and rock'n'roll with bar, food,
live DJs and comfy seats
accompanying each talk.

Dartington *July*
*www.wayswithwords.co.uk
/dartington.html*
Vibrant ten-day festival in the
grounds of the famously
progressive Dartington school.

Port Eliot Lit Fest *July*
www.porteliotlitfest.com
It's 'Glastonbury for books'
except you get to pitch your tents
in the magnificent grounds of
Port Eliot for free.

Folkestone Literary Festival *Sept*
www.folkestonelitfest.com
Literary giants, brilliant sunshine
and a lively audience, this is a
festival with an essentially
Kentish character.

Southwold *November*
*www.wayswithwords.co.uk/south
wold.html*
Relaxed beachside celebration of
all things literary.

When www.straightdope.com asked its readers what *The Lord of the Rings* would have sounded like if it had been written by someone else, they received an avalanche of prose and song parodies. Here are some of the best...

JD Salinger

When Gandalf told me that Gollum used to be a hobbit, I just got so depressed all of a sudden. I really did. I mean, if he's supposed to be a hobbit, why can't he just BE one? People should just stay what they are and not go changing into goddamn slimey reptile creatures. To be honest, this whole ring thing was really making me depressed as hell. The quest was giving me a big pain in the ass. If anyone ever tries to give you an all powerful ring, don't take it, it will only make you more depressed, I swear to God.

Lewis Carroll

Frodo was beginning to get very tired of living with his uncle Bilbo in Hobbiton and of having nothing to do: once or twice he had peeped into the red book in which Bilbo was writing, but he couldn't make it out and it did not have enough pictures of elves, 'and what is the use of a book,' thought Frodo 'without pictures of elves?' So he was considering in his own mind (as well as he could, for the hot day made him feel very sleepy), whether the pleasure of having an ale with Sam in Bywater would be worth the trouble of getting up, when suddenly a dwarf with a blue hood and walking stick ran close by him. There was nothing so very remarkable in that; nor did Frodo think it so very much out of the way to hear the Dwarf say to himself, 'Oh dear! Oh dear! I shall be late! And Balin will be so angry with me' (when he thought it over afterwards, it occurred to him that he ought to have wondered at this, but at the time it all seemed quite natural); but when the dwarf took out a large axe and swung it a few times, and then hurried on, Frodo started to his feet, for it flashed across his mind that he had never before seen a Dwarf in Hobbiton with either an axe or a belt to remove it from, and burning with curiosity, he ran across the field after it, and fortunately was just in time to see it pop down a large hole under the hedge.

Mark Twain

You don't know about me without you have read a book by the name of *The Red Book of Westmarch;* but that ain't no matter. That book was made by Mr Frodo Baggins and his Uncle Bilbo, and they told the truth, mainly. There was things which they stretched, but mostly they told the truth. That is nothing. I never seen anybody but lied one time or another, without it was the Lady Galadriel, or Elrond, or maybe Gandalf. The Lady Galadriel and others is all told about in that book, which is mostly a true book, with some stretchers, as I said before.

QUOTE UNQUOTE

Read the best books first, or you may not
have a chance to read them at all.
Henry David Thoreau, US poet and author

WRITERS ON WRITING

When young one builds up habits of work that one believes will last a lifetime and withstand any catastrophe. Over twenty years I have probably averaged five hundred words a day for five days a week. I can produce a novel in a year, and that allows time for revision and the correction of the typescript. I have always been very methodical and when my quota of work is done, I break off even in the middle of a scene. Every now and then during the morning's work I count what I have done and mark off the hundreds on my manuscript. No printer need make a careful cast-off of my work, for there on my typescript is marked the figure – 83, 764. When I was young not even a love affair would alter my schedule. A love affair had to begin after lunch, and however late I might be in getting to bed - so long as I slept in my own bed – I would read the morning's work over and sleep on it.

Graham Greene, *The End of The Affair*

HITLER'S FORGOTTEN LIBRARY

He may be better known for burning books than collecting them, but some of the books from Adolf Hitler's personal library are now housed in the rare-book reading room of the Library of Congress. Among the 1,200 books in the Third Reich Collection can be found...

Death and Immortality in the World View of Indo-Germanic Thinkers, inscribed for Hitler by SS chief Heinrich Himmler

Don Quixote, Miguel de Cervantes

German Essays, Paul de Lagarde

Gulliver's Travels, Jonathan Swift

Mein Kampf, Adolf Hitler

Robinson Crusoe, Daniel Defoe

The Predictions of Nostradamus

The World as Will and Representation, Schopenhauer

Uncle Tom's Cabin, Harriet Beecher Stowe

Winnetou, Old Surehand and *Bad Guy*, Karl May

A French vegetarian cookbook with an inscription from its author, Maïa Charpentier

ENGLISH LITERATURE IN PERIODS

For convenience of discussion, historians divide the continuity of English literature into segments of time called 'periods'...

450–1066 *Old English (or Anglo-Saxon Period)*
What to Read: Beowulf (eighth century)

1066–1500 *Middle English Period*
Chaucer's The Canterbury Tales

1500–1660 *The Renaissance*

1558–1603 *Elizabethan Age*
Shakespeare, Christopher Marlowe, Ben Jonson

1603–25 *Jacobean Age*
Shakespeare's tragedies, John Donne, John Webster

1625–49 *Caroline Age*
John Milton, the Cavalier poets – Richard Lovelace, Sir John Suckling and Thomas Carew

1649–60 *Commonwealth Period (also known as the Puritan Interregnum)*
Andrew Marvell

1660–1785 *The Neoclassical Period*

1660–1700 *The Restoration*
William Congreve and John Dryden

1700–1745 *The Augustan Age (or Age of Pope)*
Alexander Pope, Jonathan Swift and Daniel Defoe

1745–85 *The Age of Sensibility (or Age of Johnson)*
Samuel Johnson, Oliver Goldsmith and James Boswell

1785–1830 *The Romantic Period*
William Wordsworth, Samuel Taylor Coleridge, Percy Bysshe Shelley, John Keats, Jane Austen, Anne Radcliffe

1832–1901 *The Victorian Period*
Tennyson, Robert Browning, Elizabeth Barrett Browning, John Ruskin, Charles Dickens, William Makepeace Thackery, the Brontë Sisters, Thomas Hardy

1848–60 *The Pre-Raphaelites*
Dante Gabriel Rossetti

1880–1901 *Aestheticism and Decadence*
Oscar Wilde

1901–1914 *The Edwardian Period*
Thomas Hardy, WB Yeats, Joseph Conrad, HG Wells, Rudyard Kipling

1910–36 *The Georgian Period*
Rupert Brooke, Walter de la Mare

1914– *The Modern Period*
TS Eliot, WH Auden, Robert Graves, Dylan Thomas, James Joyce, DH Lawrence, Virginia Woolf, EM Forster, Graham Greene, Doris Lessing, Samuel Beckett...

150 *The number, in millions, of items in the British Library collection on publication of this book*

Added an extra 17 feet of bookshelves to their homes

Fell asleep in nine different libraries

Read *Ulysses* from cover to cover and prepared eloquent discourse on the Joycean perspective

Thought they saw Martin Amis at Heathrow airport once, but he was a long way off, and his back was turned, and come to think of it he looked a little tall, so in retrospect it might have been someone else

Worked out that the average novel length among those they had read was 273 pages and 17 words

Read tonnes of sonnet anthologies, then realised that the two words are anagrams of each other

Wondered if any poet had ever been more aptly named than Wordsworth

Read *Pincher Martin*, only to find the last page was missing

Started to write a very good short story, but couldn't decide which word to use at the

Figured that if a Grecian Urns enough, then it doesn't matter what he's Ode

Bought 11 first editions off ebay

Lied about the *Ulysses* thing

Please note that although every effort has been made to ensure accuracy in this book, the above statistics may be the result of tall-tale-telling minds.

There are books of which the backs and covers are by far the best parts.

Charles Dickens, novelist

The answers. As if you needed them.

P13.   Thomas Hardy, Emily Brontë, TS Eliot and Edgar Allan Poe

P20.   The authors are all thought to have had careers as spies.

P29.   They all set novels in trains: *Murder on the Orient Express* (Agatha Christie), *The Great Train Robbery* (Michael Crichton), *Stamboul Train* (Graham Greene) and *The Railway Children* (E Nesbit).

P34.   Myshkin

P36.   1. *Wuthering Heights*, Emily Brontë (1845–1847)
        2. *Little Women*, Louisa May Alcott (1868–1869)
        3. *Tropic of Cancer*, Henry Miller (1934)
        4. *Lord of the Flies*, William Golding (1954)
        5. *Catch-22*, Joseph Heller (1961)
        6. *A Clockwork Orange*, Anthony Burgess (1962)
        7. *The Satanic Verses*, Salman Rushdie (1988)
        8. *Crime and Punishment*, Fyodor Dostoevsky (1866)
        9. *Animal Farm*, George Orwell (1945)
        10. *Anna Karenina*, Leo Tolstoy (1873-7)
        11. *The Trial*, Franz Kafka (1925)
        12. *Jane Eyre*, Charlotte Brontë (1847)
        13. *The Pilgrim's Progress*, John Bunyan (1678)
        14. *The Secret Garden*, Frances Hodgson Burnett (1911)
        15. *Through the Looking Glass... and What Alice Found There*, Lewis Carroll (1872)
        16. *David Copperfield*, Charles Dickens (1849-50)
        17. *1984*, George Orwell (1949)
        18. *Lady Chatterley's Lover*, DH Lawrence (1928)

P44.   They have all appeared in cameo roles in the film adaptations of their books: JG Ballard (*Empire of the Sun*), Robert Harling (*Steel Magnolias*), Stephen King (*Pet Cemetery*, among others) and Irvine Welsh (*Trainspotting*).

P57.   Seven: *Agnes Grey* and *The Tenant of Wildfell Hall* (Anne); *The Professor, Jane Eyre, Shirley* and *Villette* (Charlotte); and *Wuthering Heights* (Emily).

P63.   Although usually associated with the Queen in *Alice's Adventures in Wonderland*, the phrase actually originated in Shakespeare's *Richard III* (Act III, scene iv) when Richard of Gloucester (as he was then) sentenced Lord Hastings to death with the words: 'Thou art a traitor: off with his head!'

Number of copies, in thousands, that Hemingway's The Old Man and the Sea *153 sold within two days of it's publication in book form*

POETIC PUZZLERS

P70.   (Joseph) Conrad

P74.   Griffin

P88.   *David Copperfield*. In 1868 he wrote: 'Of all my books, I like this the best. It will be easily believed that I am a fond parent of every child of my fancy, and that no one can ever love a family as dearly as I love them. But, like many fond parents, I have in my heart of hearts a favourite child. And his name is *David Copperfield*.'

P91.   Mersault

P99.   Oliver Mellors

P108. Antonio

P119. WB Yeats

P123. Dr Charles Primrose

P135. 1. 'Snake', DH Lawrence
2. 'Dulce et Decorum Est', Willfred Owen
3. 'Do Not Go Gentle Into That Good Night', Dylan Thomas
4. 'Composed Upon Westminster Bridge', William Wordsworth
5. Sonnet 42: 'How do I love thee? Let me count the ways', Elizabeth Barrett Browning
6. 'Ozymandias of Egypt', Percy Bysshe Shelley
7. 'Macavity: The Mystery Cat', TS Eliot
8. 'A Red, Red Rose', Robert Burns
9. 'Cargoes', John Masefield
10. 'Ode To Autumn', John Keats
11. 'Elegy Written in a Country Churchyard', Thomas Gray
12. 'The Tyger', William Blake
13. 'Leisure', WH Daview

P141. Sarah Woodruff

FURTHER READING

ABC of Reading, Ezra Pound

The Anatomy of Bibliomania, Holbrook Jackson

The A-Z of Almost Everything, Trevor Montague

Bizarre Books, edited by Russell Ash and Brian Lake

Brewer's Concise Phrase & Fable, edited by
Betty Kirkpatrick

The Cassell Dictionary of Clichés, Nigel Rees

Ex Libris: Confessions of a Common Reader, Anne Fadiman

Longman Quotation Guide

The Oxford Companion to English Literature, edited by
Margaret Drabble

The Top Ten of Everything 2004, Russell Ash

Writers at Work, edited by George Plimpton

ACKNOWLEDGEMENTS

We gratefully acknowledge permission to reprint extracts of copyright material in this book from the following authors, publishers and executors:

Extract from *Captain Corelli's Mandolin* by Louis de Bernières published by Vintage (May 1995). Used by permission of The Random House Group Limited.

Approximately 403 words from *Ex Libris, Confessions Of A Common Reader* by Anne Fadiman (Penguin Press, 2000) Copyright © Anne Fadiman, 2000

The End of the Affair, Graham Greene, published by Random House by kind permission of David Higham Associates.

Revelations, Bill Hicks, by kind permission of Arizona Bay Production Co Inc.

John Humphrys, Introduction to *Between You and I: A Little Book of Bad English*, James Cochrane, by kind permission of Icon Books.

Mortification, Writers' Stories of their Public Shame, Glyn Maxwell, edited by Robin Robertson, reprinted by permission of HarperCollins Publishers Ltd. (c) Robin Robertson, 2004.

OTHER TITLES AVAILABLE IN THE SERIES

The Cook's Companion
Whether your taste is for foie gras or fry-ups, this tasty compilation is an essential ingredient in any kitchen, boiling over with foodie facts, fiction, science, history and trivia.
ISBN 1-86105-772-5

The Gardener's Companion
For anyone who has ever put on a pair of gloves, picked up a spade and gone out into the garden in search of flowers, beauty and inspiration.
ISBN 1-86105-771-7

The London Companion
From Edgware to Morden, Upminster to Ealing, here's your chance to explore the history, mystery and many peculiarities of the most exciting capital city in the world.
ISBN 1-86105-799-7

The Moviegoer's Companion
Explore the strange and wonderful world of movies, actors, cinemas and salty popcorn in all their glamorous glory from film noir to Matt LeBlanc.
ISBN 1-86105-797-0

The Politics Companion
The history, myths, great leaders and greater liars of international politics are all gathered around the hustings in this remarkable compilation. This is the book that finally makes politics tick.
ISBN 1-86105-796-2

The Traveller's Companion
For anyone who's ever stared at a distant plane, wondered where it's going, and spent the rest of the day dreaming of faraway lands and ignoring everything and everyone else.
ISBN 1-86105-773-3

The Walker's Companion
If you've ever laced a sturdy boot, packed a cheese and pickle sandwich, and put one foot in front of the other in search of stimulation and contemplation, then this book is for you.
ISBN 1-86105-825-X

The Wildlife Companion
Animal amazements, ornithological oddities and botanical beauties abound in this compilation of natural need-to-knows and nonsense for wildlife-lovers everywhere.
ISBN 1-86105-770-9